S+B
90970
12/97
10·95

YORK NOTES

General Editors: Professor A.N. Jeffares (*University of Stirling*) & Professor Suheil Bushrui (*American University of Beirut*)

Margaret Atwood

THE HANDMAID'S TALE

Notes by Coral Ann Howells

MA (QUEENSLAND), PH D (LONDON)
Reader in Canadian Literature, University of Reading

LONGMAN
YORK PRESS

D0009532

ACKNOWLEDGEMENTS
The author wishes to thank Margaret Atwood for permission to quote from *The Handmaid's Tale* and from manuscript materials, and also Maureen Boyd of Langley Grammar School, Berkshire, and Constance Rooke, Chair of the English Department, University of Guelph, Canada, for their valuable assistance in the preparation of these Notes. Thanks are due also to the author's daughters Phoebe and Miranda, who read through the typescript with the acutely critical eyes that only teenage students possess.

YORK PRESS
Immeuble Esseily, Place Riad Solh, Beirut

ADDISON WESLEY LONGMAN LIMITED
Edinburgh Gate, Harlow,
Essex CM20 2JE, England
Associated companies, branches and representatives
throughout the world

First published 1993
Seventh impression 1997

ISBN 0-582-21538-2

Phototypeset by Intype, London
Printed in Singapore

Contents

Part 1

Introduction

The life and works of Margaret Atwood

Margaret Atwood is a Canadian writer whose work is so well known internationally that readers tend to forget that she is Canadian. Atwood herself never forgets this, and her writing is grounded in a strong sense of her cultural identity as a Canadian and a woman. These are not, however, limiting categories, for her writing challenges boundaries of nationality and gender in its explorations of what it means to be a human being. As she wrote in 1982: 'If writing novels – and reading them – have any redeeming social value, it's probably that they force you to imagine what it's like to be somebody else. Which increasingly is something we all need to know.'[*]

Margaret Atwood is now in her early fifties. Born in Ottawa in 1939, she spent her early childhood moving around rural Ontario and Quebec with her family, as her father was a field entomologist. In 1946 he became a university professor in Toronto, and the family settled there. Margaret Atwood spent her schooldays in Toronto and began writing poetry and prose for the school magazine. When she was an undergraduate studying English at the University of Toronto she was busy writing and reviewing for college magazines and designing programmes for the drama society. In 1961, the year that she graduated, she had her first book published, a collection of poems entitled *Double Persephone*. Atwood's first experience of the United States of America was in 1961 when she went as a graduate student to Harvard University, where she studied American literature, learned a great deal about seventeenth-century Puritan New England, and realised how little the Americans knew about Canada. She did not stay to finish her Ph D, but during the 1960s she moved around a lot, working briefly in market research in Toronto, teaching English at several universities across Canada, making her first trip to Europe, returning for two years to Harvard, getting married, and writing the draft of her first novel *The Edible Woman* (published in 1969, in Canada, the USA and Britain). In 1965 she won Canada's major literary prize, the Governor-General's Award, for her collection of poems *The Circle Game*.

[*]M. Atwood, 'Writing the Male Character', in *Second Words: Selected Critical Prose*, Anansi, Toronto, 1982, p. 430.

By the age of thirty-two, Atwood was quite sure that she was going to become a successful writer, and she was extremely productive in the 1970s, publishing three novels – *Surfacing* (1972), *Lady Oracle* (1976), *Life Before Man* (1977); five books of poetry – *The Journals of Susanna Moodie* (1970), *Procedures for Underground* (1970), *Power Politics* (1971), *You Are Happy* (1974) and *Two-Headed Poems* (1978); a book of short stories – *Dancing Girls* (1979); a major work of literary criticism – *Survival: A Thematic Guide to Canadian Literature* (1972); and a children's book – *Up in the Tree* (1978). In addition she frequently designed the covers for her own books and wrote a comic strip cartoon for *Ms* magazine. After her brief first marriage, Atwood's relationship with Canadian novelist Graeme Gibson began, and their daughter was born in 1976. As her literary reputation grew, Atwood began travelling extensively to give readings and lectures, visiting Britain, Italy, Australia and Afghanistan in the late 1970s; she also won many literary prizes.

The pattern of family life with a home in Toronto combined with high productivity, international travel and acclaim has continued through the 1980s into the 1990s. Her output as poet, novelist and critic has been prodigious, frequently at the rate of more than one book per year: *True Stories* (poetry) and *Bodily Harm* (novel) (1981); *Second Words: Selected Critical Prose* (1982); *Murder in the Dark* (prose poems) and *Bluebeard's Egg* (short stories) (1983); *Interlunar* (poems) (1984); *The Handmaid's Tale* (novel) (1985); *Selected Poems II* (1986); *The Can Lit Food Book* (1987); *Cat's Eye* (novel) (1988); *Margaret Atwood: Conversations* (1990); *Wilderness Tips* (short stories) (1991); *Good Bones* (short fictions) (1992); and *The Robber Bride* (novel) (1993). She has also edited *The Oxford Book of Canadian Verse in English* (1982) and co-edited *The Oxford Book of Short Stories in English* (1986).

Clearly, Margaret Atwood is dazzlingly proficient in both poetry and prose. Confining our attention to her eight novels, we see her experimenting with a range of traditional narratives from Gothic romances and fairy-tales to spy thrillers, science fiction utopias and fictive autobiographies. *The Handmaid's Tale* combines elements from all these, for if one of the distinctive features of her fiction is its experimentalism, another is its continuities. Margaret Atwood has always believed that art has a social function: 'What art does, it takes what society deals out and makes it visible, right? So you can see it' (as her male porn artist declares in *Bodily Harm*). From *The Edible Woman* onwards, her novels have been eye-witness (I-witness) accounts which focus on contemporary political issues: 'And what do we mean by "political"? What we mean is how people relate to a power structure and vice versa.'* This wide definition of 'politics' accommodates all of Atwood's enduring concerns: her scrutiny of male–female relationships and cultural myths about women, her ecological interests, her nationalist concern with relations between Canada and the United States, and her wider humanitarian concerns with totalitarian regimes and forms of state oppression.

The Handmaid's Tale has been Margaret Atwood's most popular novel. (It was made into a film in 1990, with a screenplay by Harold Pinter, starring Natasha Richardson, Faye Dunaway and Robert Duvall.) This is perhaps surprising, for the tale presents a bleak scenario of the future, belonging, like George Orwell's *Nineteen Eighty-Four*, to the genre of anti-utopian science fiction. Published in 1985, it might be read as a feminist update of *Nineteen Eighty-Four*, since its Republic of Gilead, set up in what was formerly New England, is a totalitarian regime run on militarist and patriarchal lines deriving from seventeenth-century American Puritanism and Old Testament principles. In this fundamentalist society individual freedom is abolished, and everyone is in service to the state; dissidents are brutally suppressed, and there is strict censorship and border control. This is an exposure of power politics at their most basic – 'Who can do what to whom', as Offred the narrator says. Indeed, it is women who are worst off, for they are valued only in terms of their biological usefulness as child bearers in a society where the birth rate has fallen to a catastrophically low level. Atwood's feminist concerns are plain, but so are her concerns for basic human rights, and the novel is a strong warning against current political trends and environmental pollution. As she said in London in 1986: 'If you see someone walking towards a hole in the ground and you want them to fall in, you don't *say* anything.'

Gilead is frightening because it presents a mirror image of contemporary Western crises, only slightly distorted to invent a nightmare future. It is Margaret Atwood's version of 'What if?' in the most powerful democracy in the world. She describes her anti-utopian project precisely in an unpublished essay '*The Handmaid's Tale* – Before and After':

> It's set in the near future, in a United States which is in the hands of a power-hungry elite who have used their own brand of 'Bible-based' religion as an excuse for the suppression of the majority of the population. It's about what happens at the intersection of several trends, all of which are with us today: the rise of right-wing fundamentalism as a political force, the decline of the Caucasian birth rate in North America and northern Europe, the rise

---

*Quoted in *Margaret Atwood: Conversations*, Virago, London, 1992, p. 185.

in infertility and birth-defect rates, due, some say, to increased chemical pollutant and radiation levels, as well as to sexually transmitted diseases.*

As Atwood has said repeatedly in the novel and outside it, there is nothing here which has not been done already by somebody, somewhere. However it is as a social critique of the 1980s and a political fable for our time that *The Handmaid's Tale* is uncannily accurate. When she began thinking about the book in 1981, she kept a clippings file of items from newspapers and magazines which contributed directly to her writing. These show Atwood's wide-ranging historical and humanitarian interests, where pamphlets from Friends of the Earth and Greenpeace sit beside reports of atrocities in Latin America, Iran and the Philippines, together with cuttings on surrogate mothers, forms of institutional control of human reproduction from Nazi Germany to Ceausescu's Romania, plus a warning given by a Canadian feminist sociologist on threats to women from new reproductive technologies.

Gilead has a specifically American location, and the clippings file contains a great deal of material on the American New Right in the early 1980s, with its warnings about the 'Birth Dearth', its pro-natalism, and its religious underpinnings in the Bible Belt. As a coalition of conservative interests which sought to influence government legislation on family issues and public morals, the New Right harked back to America's Puritan inheritance, supporting Ronald Reagan as 'the most evangelical President since the Founding Fathers'. Though no longer called 'New', the extreme Right was still in evidence during the 1992 Presidential election campaign, fighting the same struggle for 'the soul of America'. It is this assault on liberal social policies that is satirised in *The Handmaid's Tale*, for Gilead represents an extreme version of such ideology in practice. Taking the point a step further, we might read the novel as an oblique form of Canadian–American dialogue, where a Canadian writer warns the Americans and where Canada is the place over the border in the north to which Offred hopes to make her escape from Gilead.

Gilead's attempts to strip women of their individuality and to redefine female identity in reductively biological terms provides the opportunity for a scrutiny of North American feminism in its recent history. As a feminist with a great distrust of ideological hardlines, Atwood refuses to simplify the debate or to swallow slogans whole. Instead she questions the possible meanings of the 60s feminist catch-

*This material is in the Atwood manuscripts held in the Fisher Rare Book Room at the University of Toronto.

phrase 'a women's culture', while chronicling one woman's story of resistance to patriarchal tyranny. All the women in the novel are survivors of the time before Gilead, so their voices represent different feminine and feminist positions dating back to the Women's Liberation Movement of the 1960s and 70s. Offred's mother belongs to this activist group with its campaigns for women's sexual freedom and its book burnings of pornography. The heroines of this era were Simone de Beauvoir, Betty Friedan and Germaine Greer. The feminist movement rapidly gained strength in the United States, winning Congressional endorsement of the Equal Rights Amendment in 1972 and the Supreme Court decision to make abortion legal in 1973, despite opposition by fundamentalist Christians and Pro-Life campaigners. The opponents to feminism are represented in the novel by the Commander's Wife and the Aunts, who show they are more than willing to collaborate with Gilead's regime to re-educate women back into traditional gender roles. Among the Handmaids, younger women who grew up in the 1970s and 80s, positions are equally varied, from those who accept the female victim role, to radicals such as the lesbian feminist Moira, who escapes from the care of the Aunts. There is also Offred, who tells this story of female resistance and who highlights the paradoxes and dilemmas within contemporary feminism.

The novel is, then, a critique of feminism, though it could not be called anti-feminist. It is clear where its sympathies lie, and arguably Offred's values can be said to offer an alternative to the male-dominated system of Gilead. Atwood is warning that some radical feminist positions and slogans run the risk of being taken over by a dominant power group, only to be exploited as a new instrument of female oppression (even with female collaborators). She also insists that feminists have never marched under a single banner: 'As for Woman, capital W, we got stuck with that for centuries. Eternal woman. But really, "Woman" is the sum total of women. It doesn't exist apart from that, except as an abstracted idea.'* It is Offred, the witty, sceptical woman who cares about men, about mother–daughter relationships and about her female friends, who survives to tell her story.

The main difficulties with *The Handmaid's Tale* lie not in the language itself, which is simple and direct, but in the numerous biblical allusions that are woven into the official Gileadean rhetoric. Many of these allusions are explained in the 'Detailed summaries' that follow, but it may be a good idea for the reader sometimes to consult a biblical concordance (the 'Suggestions for further reading'

Conversations, p. 201.

section, p. 87, gives details of two standard concordances) and to read the Bible. Another difficulty lies in the fragmented narrative design. This will be discussed in Part 3, p. 43.

A note on the text

The Handmaid's Tale was first published in hardback in 1985 in Canada (McClelland & Stewart, Toronto). The following year it was published in hardback in Britain and the United States (Jonathan Cape, London; and Houghton Mifflin, Boston). Published in paperback in Britain by Virago Press Ltd., London, in 1987, it has been reprinted several times. The edition used in the preparation of these notes is the currently available Virago paperback, and there are several other paperback editions published in Canada and the United States.

Part 2

Summaries
of THE HANDMAID'S TALE

A general summary

This anti-utopian fable about the future is one woman's story of her life as a Handmaid in the Republic of Gilead. As a Handmaid in the Old Testament sense, whose body is at the service of the patriarchs, Offred the narrator has been deprived of her own name and legal rights. Assigned to a particular Commander for reproductive purposes, she is a virtual prisoner in his household, under constant surveillance from his Wife and the female servants. She is also forbidden to read and write or to form any close personal friendships. Her only outings are daily shopping expeditions with another Handmaid and compulsory attendance at public events such as Prayvaganzas, Birth Days and Salvagings. Once a month, she has to undergo the grotesque impregnation Ceremony with the Commander in the presence of his Wife. She continually lives in fear of being sent to the Colonies as an Unwoman if she does not conceive a child.

Trapped in such a circumscribed existence, what kind of freedom could a woman possibly have? Offred chooses the freedom of refusal: she refuses to believe in Gileadean doctrines, she refuses to forget her past life, and crucially she refuses to be silenced. Reading the novel induces a kind of double vision, for Offred is always facing both ways as she tells her story, shifting constantly between the present and the past. We learn about the Commander and their 'out of hours' relationship where they play Scrabble and she is allowed to read, and we learn about her illicit love affair with Nick, the Commander's chauffeur. Looking backward, Offred tells us about her lost husband Luke and their daughter and about her mother and her college friend Moira.

Against the odds and in the very face of tyranny and persecution in public life, Offred manages to tell a witty dissident tale of private lives and personal relationships, which also includes the secret stories of other women. There is the story of Moira, the rebel who manages to escape the power of the Aunts and who later reappears working at Jezebel's, the high-class brothel for army officers and foreign businessmen; there is the story fragment of Offred's nameless predecessor at the Commander's house who leaves a hidden message on the wall and then hangs herself from the light fitting. There are also stories about the Commander's Wife who used to be a television personality on a gospel show, as well as bits of gossip from the female servants and the other Wives. Offred creates a mosaic of alternative female worlds which deny patriarchal myths of women's submissiveness and silence. If women are marginal to the masculine world of public power struggles, men are shown to exist only on the periphery of this 'women's culture'. There are soldiers and guardians, there are the dead bodies of male dissidents hanging on the Wall, and there are occasional more intimate night-time encounters, but this is a story focused on women's bodies and their domestic lives.

At the end, Offred makes her exit from the Commander's house in the black van kept to cart dissidents away. Her escape seems to have been arranged by Nick and the underground resistance movement, but Offred does not know whether she will manage to escape over the border to Canada or whether she will be taken to prison. Her voice stops when she climbs up into the van, so we never hear the end of her story, just as she never hears the end of Moira's or her mother's or Luke's story. This novel is full of Missing Persons.

There is an epilogue to Offred's story in the Historical Notes. This is presented as the transcription of an academic paper delivered at a Symposium on Gileadean Studies in the year 2195. Atwood adopts a 'fast forward' technique here, leaping two hundred years ahead into a future beyond Gilead. By that time, of course, Offred is dead and Gilead itself has fallen. The paper fills in a lot of background information about Gilead and how Offred's story came to be discovered, but it also challenges us as readers on questions of interpretation. After the audience have applauded the paper there comes the signal for opening up discussion: 'Are there any questions?' The novel ends not as academic speculation on the past but as a challenge to its readers in the present.

Detailed summaries

NOTE: *The Handmaid's Tale* is divided into fifteen named sections, which are subdivided into forty-eight chapters. These chapters in turn are divided into several scenic units marked by gaps in the text. There is also an unnumbered final section called 'Historical Notes'. This structure indicates that the text will be a rather fragmented narrative.

Prefatory material

This is a novel in which the prefatory material suggests some possible approaches to the tale. Who were the two dedicatees? And what is the significance of the three quotations which form the Epigraph?

Mary Webster was one of Atwood's Puritan ancestors. She was hanged as a witch in Connecticut in 1683, but she survived the hanging and was allowed to go free. Like Offred, she was a woman who successfully flouted the law of the Puritan state.

Professor Perry Miller was Atwood's Director of American Studies at Harvard. His two books, *The New England Mind: The Seventeenth Century* (1939) and *The New England Mind: From Colony to Province* (1953), have made his reputation as an authority on Puritan history.

While these two names hint at the Puritan background used for Gilead, the three quotations give us other useful information.

The first quotation, from Genesis 30:1–3, is the Old Testament story of surrogate mothers on which the novel is based. It also provides the biblical rationale for the patriarchal state of Gilead.

The second quotation is from Jonathan Swift's *A Modest Proposal* (1729), a desperate plea for improving conditions in Ireland in the 1720s in the form of a ferocious pamphlet recommending cannibalism and the treatment of women and children as cattle. In using it, Atwood signals, at the very opening of the book, her thematic and satiric intentions.

The third quotation, taken from a Sufi proverb suggests that, in the natural world, the human instinct for survival can be trusted. It is a comment on the polluted world of Gilead where the balance of nature has been destroyed, and is also an implied criticism of the state's over-regulation of human social and sexual activities.

Section 1. Chapter 1

'Night' is the title of the opening section, and 'Night' recurs as a section heading seven times, including the final section. It always signals 'time out', when Offred's life is not under glaring public scrutiny and when she can thus escape into her private world of memory and desire.

It is night-time, but we do not know who the narrator is, or where she is. All we know is that she is one of a group of young women who are being held in a makeshift prison camp in what was once a college gymnasium, controlled by two women gaolers ironically called Aunts, with heavy guard outside. The narrator nostalgically recalls the games and the dances that used to be held here between the 1960s and 1980s. It sounds very like an American campus, which indeed it turns out to be. This is, or was, Harvard University, which has undergone a striking transformation.

This short chapter manages to evoke both regimental discipline and the young women's ability to evade it when the Aunts are not looking. The chapter ends with a whispered list of first names, and, of course, we wonder which one is the narrator's. (During the story, all but one name is assigned to someone. Do you think the narrator's real name could be June?)

In this novel the narrator is not addressed by any name until Chapter 24. She is then called by her Gileadean name 'Offred', so for clarity this name will be used throughout the chapter summaries.

NOTES AND GLOSSARY:

electric cattle prods: electrified pointed instruments used to control cattle, but also used by the police in US civil rights and race riots of the late 1960s. Here the term makes explicit the association between these women and breeding animals

Angels: soldiers of Gilead's army, who fight in battalions with names like 'Angels of the Apocalypse' and 'Angels of Light'. They wear black uniforms. The name is possibly also linked with the New York 'guardian angels', a paramilitary force used to curb social violence

---

Section 2. Chapter 2

Under the section heading 'Shopping' which describes the daily domestic routines of the Handmaids, Offred begins to piece together her present situation, building up her account through short scenes and fragments of memory.

She is alone in a single bedroom in an old-fashioned house, where she is virtually kept a prisoner. Her actions seem to follow a prescribed pattern and her old-fashioned red dress and white headgear signal her membership of a group. But what does the red dress ('the colour of blood') stand for? The house belongs to a mysterious Commander and his Wife and there are female servants, but Offred is obviously isolated from them. She is assigned to do the shopping, and her role seems to be connected to having babies. There is also one reference to a man named Luke whom she remembers with affection.

NOTES AND GLOSSARY:

return to traditional values: a reference to Gilead's reactionary social ethos, which confines women to the home and to domestic roles

Martha:	female domestic servant in Gilead, from the biblical story of Martha and Mary; see Luke 10:38–42. In this society, it will be noted that almost all the characters are designated by their roles, for example, Commander, Wife, Aunt, Handmaid
Colonies:	places on the borders of Gilead to which dissidents are sent to clear up toxic waste and to die

Chapter 3

This chapter reveals Offred's role in the household: her job is to be a surrogate mother, a Handmaid, bearing a child for the Commander and his ageing Wife. This is clearly not a voluntary arrangement but the result of a government order.

Beginning in the present, where she walks through the luxuriant garden hoping not to meet the Wife, the focus is on Offred's first meeting with this woman five weeks earlier when she had been delivered at her new 'posting'. There is a strong contrast drawn between the two women, one young and dressed in red, and the other old and dressed in pale blue. The older woman is powerful and antagonistic, and the younger one is constantly reminded of her inferiority and of the danger threatening her if she does not obey the rules. Yet there is a strange revelation at the end, for Offred remembers that the Wife was formerly a television personality on a gospel show and was called Serena Joy. She also realises that this woman too is now trapped like herself in a patriarchal system which rigidly controls all women.

NOTES AND GLOSSARY:

Guardian:	member of the Gileadean police force. Guardians wear green uniforms and their official title is 'Guardians of the Faith'
Scriptural precedent:	the first direct textual reference to Genesis 30:1–3 and to the Handmaid's role as slave and surrogate mother

Chapter 4

In this chapter, with its switch back to the present, Offred first meets Nick, the Commander's chauffeur, and Ofglen, her shopping companion. Nick clearly does not toe the Party line, and when he winks at Offred, she senses that here is somebody who is as dissident as herself. By contrast, Ofglen seems totally devoid of personality, but on reflection, Offred decides that this may be out of fear rather than conviction, for the Handmaids are meant to spy on each other. Their bizarre walk to the shops presents the odd mixture of familiar and unfamiliar which characterises Gileadean society, where ordinary domesticity and military regimentation exist side by side. Looking at the sex-starved young soldiers at the road barrier, Offred reflects that Gilead is deeply misogynistic, working through law to censor and if possible prohibit sexual urges in men as well as in women. She also makes the point that such repression actually encourages a society-wide obsession with sex.

NOTES AND GLOSSARY:

Whirlwind: see the Bible, Jeremiah 23:19: 'Behold, a whirlwind of the Lord is gone forth in fury, even a grievous whirlwind'

Behemoth: a monstrous beast, counterpart of the sea-beast Leviathan. See the Bible, Job 40:15. Car brand names are biblical, which is typical of Gilead with its strange mix of religious fundamentalism and late twentieth-century technology

Eye: member of the secret police. See the Bible, Proverbs 15:3, and compare with the famous phrase in George Orwell's *Nineteen Eighty-Four*, 'Big Brother is watching you.' The Eyes wear grey uniforms

They also serve: last line of the sonnet 'On His Blindness' (*c.* 1654), by John Milton

Blessed be the fruit: Handmaids' ritual greetings focus on procreation; see the Bible, Genesis 1:28

Ofglen: Handmaids are known by their Commanders' first names, so as to underline their function as sexual objects without individuality

Salvagings: Gileadean public executions (see Section 14)

Prayvaganzas: Gileadean mass-religious ceremonies. Women's Prayvaganzas are for group weddings; men's Prayvaganzas celebrate military victories (see Chapter 34)

Birthmobile: red minibus used to take Handmaids to witness babies' births (see Section 8)

Chapter 5

The Handmaids' walk to the shops fills in significant details of location: this is a former university town, now the capital of Gilead. Offred recognises it all because she lived here before with Luke, her former husband. We share her condition of double vision, where the present shops with their biblical names insistently remind her of how life used to be. There are two telling scenes here: one where the pregnant Handmaid, Ofwarren (formerly Janine, whom Offred knew at the Rachel and Leah Centre described in Chapter 1) sails into the shop to the envy of the other Handmaids, and the other where Offred meets a group of Japanese tourists. With a shock she realises that their westernised clothes now look as exotic to her as hers do to them.

NOTES AND GLOSSARY:

Gilead: the fundamentalist republic of Gilead is named after a place in the Old Testament, a mountainous region east of the Jordan. (In Hebrew the name means 'heap of stones', though the region also abounded in spices and aromatic herbs.) Gilead is closely connected with the history of the patriarch Jacob, and the prophet Jeremiah was a Gileadite. As a frontier land and a citadel, 'Gilead' projects the ideal image for an embattled state, run on fundamentalist religious and patriarchal principles. See the Bible, Genesis 31:21, 37:25

Gilead is within you: see the Bible, Luke 17:21, 'the kingdom of God is within you', of which Aunt Lydia's statement is a variant

Lilies of the Field: see the Bible, Luke 12:27

Milk and Honey: see the Bible, Exodus 3:8 and 17, where the land of Canaan is described as 'a land flowing with milk and honey'

Libertheos: Atwood's name for Central American freedom fighters, based on the concept of Liberation Theology, which has been a fashionable movement among the more politically radical Roman Catholic elements in Central and South America for the past twenty years

Red Centre: Rachel and Leah Re-education Centre, where Handmaids are trained (refer back to Chapter 1). The name given to the Centre emphasises female sexuality

All Flesh: 'For all flesh is as grass'. See the Bible, 1 Peter 1:24

Chapter 6

The walk back confirms the sinister transformation of the former university campus as the Handmaids stare at the dead bodies of dissidents (doctors and scientists) hanging on the Wall. Looking at the blood-stained head bag on one of the bodies, Offred determines to try to stay sane under this tyranny by refusing to believe in the distorted versions of reality which Gilead is trying to impose. She insists on distinguishing between the significance of the colour red when it is blood and when it is the colour of flowers, just as she continues to believe in the importance of individuals. It is this effort to avoid confusion which characterises her attitude throughout the novel.

NOTES AND GLOSSARY:

Our ancestors: a reference to Gileadean seventeenth-century Puritan inheritance

memento mori: a Latin phrase, meaning 'remember you have to die'; it was often used as an epitaph on gravestones

angel-makers: a seventeenth- and eighteenth-century euphemism for abortionists

Section 3. Chapter 7

In this brief 'Night' section, as Offred lies on her bed she slips away from real life into the past, remembering the three most influential female figures in her life in three distinctly separated scenes. There is her adolescent memory of her rebellious college friend Moira, then an earlier childhood memory of going with her activist mother to a feminist pornographic book burning, and most painful of all, an agonised memory of her lost child who was taken away from her by force under the new regime.

At the end of this section, Offred for the first time draws attention to her story-telling, and the reason why she needs to do it. Like writing a letter, it is a gesture reaching beyond her own isolation, just as it is her only way to go on believing in a world outside the confines of Gilead.

NOTES AND GLOSSARY:

date rape: educational campaigns to combat date and acquaintance rape on college campuses have been a significant feature of North American life in the 1980s and 90s. These important initiatives against

	sexual assault on women are supported by women's studies centres, college administrations and government ministries of education
Date Rapé:	a pun; compare *fromage rapé*: grated cheese

Section 4. Chapter 8

Going to the doctor for a compulsory monthly check-up is the main event in this section, but 'Waiting Room' also includes other examples of 'waiting' and other examples of 'rooms'.

Life seems to be full of dreary repetition for Offred; only the weather changes as summer comes in. Yet she also notices some deviations from conformity. One day when they are looking at bodies on the Wall, Ofglen uses the word 'Mayday' (which used to be a distress signal in the Second World War). The second oddity occurs when Offred goes upstairs after shopping and sees her new Commander peering into her bedroom. As she passes him, he tries to look at her face. Both these acts are strictly out of order, and she wonders what they might mean.

NOTES AND GLOSSARY:

Mayday:	the name of the Gilead Resistance movement, and also the password used by members of this secret society. Mayday (derived from the French 'm'aidez'='help me') was the standard distress call used by the Allies in the Second World War
SOS:	a Morse code distress signal, consisting of three dots, followed by three dashes, then three more dots
something from Beethoven:	by association, Offred thinks of the Symphony No. 5 (1807) by the German composer Ludwig van Beethoven, the famous opening phrase of which sounds like the beginning of the SOS signal

Chapter 9

Back in her room, which she has begun to value as her own private space, Offred sits thinking of her unknown predecessor there, who left a secret message scrawled on the wall inside the cupboard. Though she does not know what it means, Offred keeps repeating it to herself because she is cheered by it and no longer feels so isolated. However, when she tries to find out what happened to the Handmaid before her, nobody in the house will tell her.

NOTES AND GLOSSARY:
Nolite te bastardes carborundorum: a schoolboy Latin joke which
the Commander later translates as 'Don't let the
bastards grind you down'

Chapter 10

To relieve her loneliness and boredom, Offred sings snatches of
hymns and old pop songs to herself (something which is now forbidden by the regime) and looks back with nostalgia to her student
days of social and sexual freedom with Moira. She also remembers
contemporary reports in the newspapers describing male violence
against women, and begins to reassess her old attitude of social
irresponsibility, wondering if such an attitude on the part of many
women like herself contributed to the present loss of individual
freedom in Gilead. As she turns to look out of the window, she sees
Nick and the Commander getting into the car. In an upsurge of
irritation she wishes she could throw a water bomb down from her
window, as she and Moira used to do in their college days.

NOTES AND GLOSSARY:
'Amazing grace': one of the collection of *Olney Hymns* (1779) written by John Newton (1728–1807). The tune is an
American folk hymn melody
'I feel so lonely, baby': from Elvis Presley's song 'Heartbreak Hotel'
(1956)
FAITH: one of the three primary Christian graces; see
the Bible 1 Corinthians 13:13: 'And now abideth
faith, hope, charity, these three; but the greatest
of these is charity.' There is a network of allusions
to 1 Corinthians 13 in the book, and it is worth
noting that the two cushions with HOPE and
CHARITY have disappeared. In Gilead 'hope'
appears only on tombstones (Chapter 30) and
'charity' is never mentioned except by Offred
(Chapter 19). The 'charity' described in Corinthians is not almsgiving but spiritual love

Chapter 11

The Handmaid's visit to the doctor ought to be the focus of this
section, but because Offred is present only as a female body to be
medically checked for fitness, the chapter is deliberately kept short.
In fact Offred feels like a dismembered woman, with only her torso

on display and her face behind a paper screen, and the doctor himself is only partially visible, with just the upper part of his face showing above his mask.

In another breach of the rules, the doctor offers to make her pregnant, but Offred rejects his offer as being too risky. She also recognises that the doctor might be a sexual exploiter and that he may be trying to coerce her into a male power game in which she would be nothing more than a collaborator.

NOTES AND GLOSSARY:

'Give me children, or else I die': an echo of Rachel's plea in the Bible, Genesis 30:1, but it also underlines the threat to the Handmaid's life. If she fails to produce a child this time, she will be reclassified as an Unwoman and sent to the Colonies

Chapter 12

Back at the house, Offred prepares for her monthly sexual encounter with the Commander by taking a bath. Of course, as she reflects, this is prescribed as a hygienic measure, but it is also a form of ritual purification in a society where sex is associated with sin and uncleanness.

As she lies in the bath, Offred is overwhelmed by a sense of longing for her daughter whom she has not been allowed to see for three years. She is, however, recalled to the present by Cora. As she sits in her room waiting to be summoned, she thinks about keeping her composure, for she knows that her present social identity as Handmaid is one imposed on her, denying all her rights of choice as an individual.

NOTES AND GLOSSARY:

Blessed are the meek: one of the Beatitudes (see the Bible, Luke 6:20–2), describing qualities of Christian perfection

Four digits and an eye, a passport in reverse: Gilead's tattoo which immobilises women, in contrast to the winged male eye which is the state's symbol. Compare this with the numbers tattooed on prisoners' arms in Nazi concentration camps

a made thing, not something born: this echoes the most famous sentence in Simone de Beauvoir's *The Second Sex* (1949): 'One is not born, but rather becomes a woman'

Section 5. Chapter 13

The one thing Offred has in her imprisoned condition is a lot of free time, and in this short section, as she sits waiting, she escapes her role as passive breeding animal by thinking and remembering. She remembers one compulsory rest period at the Rachel and Leah Centre when her friend Moira was brought in by the Aunts, and relishes the memory of Moira's spirited resistance against the brainwashing sessions in which Janine proved herself the most abject female victim. Offred also thinks about her body, though not in the way prescribed by Gilead. Instead, she meditates intensely on her own bodily sensations, exploring her inner space like a dark continent within her.

Sinking from meditation into sleep, Offred has two of her recurring nightmares, first her dread that Luke is dead, and then her replay of their failed escape attempt across the border to Canada. There were gunshots, Luke disappeared, and her child was dragged away from her in the snow. In this state of anxiety Offred is awakened by a bell and has to leave her room to join the Commander's household downstairs.

NOTES AND GLOSSARY:

Les Sylphides: a popular Romantic ballet, with music by Frédéric Chopin, first performed in Paris in 1909 by Diaghilev's Ballets Russes

Section 6. Chapter 14

In this section we see Gilead's version of patriarchal authority in practice in the home. As Offred explains, 'Household' means a house and its male head: 'The house is what he holds'; but there is also her ironic reference to the 'hold' of a ship (probably a slave ship).

The household assembles for family prayers in the sitting-room. First Offred, then Cora, Rita and Nick come in, followed by the Wife, Serena Joy. The room is presided over by the Wife as her traditional space, though Offred's response to this charade of old-fashioned Puritan values is to emphasise its capitalist underpinnings, and mentally to compare the ageing Wife with the withered flowers in the vase on the table. Everyone watches the news on television, although it is only state propaganda. In a country where news is either censored or fabricated, there is little chance of learning the truth.

Offred's form of private resistance is to think about her real name, which she is forbidden to use, but which she holds on to as a kind of charm in the hope that one day she will have the chance to use it again. She also recalls more of the traumatic details of her family's failed escape attempt.

NOTES AND GLOSSARY:

a parlour, the kind with spiders and flies: a reference to the nursery rhyme, 'Will you walk into my parlour? said the spider to the fly'; the context gives the room a sinister overtone

Lily of the Valley perfume: in flower lore, this flower is also known as Our Lady's Tears

till death do us part: this is part of the vow in the Christian marriage service, and very threatening here, where death awaits a Handmaid if she fails to produce a child after three postings

Children of Ham and National Homeland One: references to Gilead's racist policies; see the Bible, Genesis 10:6. Ham was black. Blacks are rounded up and 'resettled' in 'National Homelands', a term that recalls South African Apartheid policies. Gilead also practises anti-semitism, putting together schemes to 'repatriate' Jewish persons to Israel

Chapter 15

Finally the Commander comes in and Offred sees him clearly for the first time as he takes the key to unlock the Bible, for he is the only person allowed to read it. She assesses his appearance and his power, though she has her own irreverent techniques for resisting them and putting them into perspective. As the Commander drones on, reading the prescribed texts from Genesis about procreation, Offred thinks back to Moira's first attempt to escape from the Red Centre and how that time she failed and was tortured. At family prayers, Offred refuses to pray and instead she silently repeats the secret message written in her cupboard.

NOTES AND GLOSSARY:

Be fruitful and multiply: this is a quotation from the Bible, Genesis 1:28

Give me children: a quotation from the Bible, Genesis 30:1–3

Beatitudes: from the Bible, Luke 6:20–2

papier poudre: (*French*) a cosmetic: small leaves of paper impregnated with face powder

hashed browns: pancakes made of grated potato, an American food speciality

For the eyes of the Lord: from the Bible, Proverbs 15:3

Chapter 16

The monthly impregnation ceremony ('The Ceremony') is described by Offred with deliberate detachment. Her detailed physical description makes it plain that this is a prime example of the patriarchal oppression of women, where violation of one woman has been legitimised with another woman's complicity demanded. Offred and Serena Joy are both there on the same bed, as the Wife has to be witness to this sexual act. Offred is prompted to wonder which of the two of them suffers more.

Chapter 17

In this crucial chapter Offred commits her first real act of rebellion. Back in her room after the Ceremony, she feels restless as she gazes out at the moon and thinks of Luke, so she decides to transgress the arbitrarily imposed rules of the household by stealing something. She goes down to the sitting-room in the dark where she takes a withered daffodil from the vase, intending to press it and leave it as part of a chain of Handmaids' secret messages. It is on this occasion that she unexpectedly meets Nick, who has come to give her a message from the Commander. In the dark room there is a strong sense of sexual attraction between them, all the more exciting because it is forbidden and dangerous. They embrace unexpectedly and passionately, and it is all Offred can do to drag herself away in order to stagger back quietly to her own room.

NOTES AND GLOSSARY:

Rachel and Leah Centre: Rachel and Leah were sisters who became wives of Jacob. Both gave their handmaids to him, so that he had children by all of these women. See the Bible, Genesis 29:16 and 30:1–3, 9–12

Section 7. Chapter 18

Back in her room and thoroughly roused, Offred remembers lying in bed with Luke before their daughter was born and contrasts this memory with her present solitary state. She tries to imagine what might have happened to Luke: is he dead, or alive in prison, or did he actually manage to escape? Kept in total ignorance, all Offred can do is to hope; that is the greatest power of resistance which she has.

Section 8. Chapter 19

A 'Birth Day' is a climactic domestic event in Gilead, and the account of the birth of Ofwarren's (Janine's) baby is a grotesquely comic mixture of a birthday party celebration and a description of natural childbirth.

The chapter opens with Offred's dreams of being somewhere else with her daughter or her mother, and her desolate awakening in her room as usual. However, her calm is shattered by the unexpected sound of the siren of the Birthmobile, which announces that the time has come for one of the Handmaids' compulsory outings: they have to go to participate in the birth of other Handmaids' babies, and on this occasion it is Janine's. In the red van on the way to the birth, Offred gives a frightening potted history of late twentieth-century environmental pollution and natural disasters, showing why the birth rate has plummeted, and indeed why Gilead could have come about.

Guarded by soldiers with machine guns, Offred and the other Handmaids file into the home of Ofwarren's Commander and his Wife; Gilead dictates that all births should take place at home by natural childbirth methods, in the presence of women only. As Offred notes with some scepticism, Gilead's emphasis on natural childbirth embraces also the idea that the pains of childbirth are women's just punishment for Eve's Original Sin. The system also generates envy and hostility between women, keeping them divided and therefore powerless.

NOTES AND GLOSSARY:

San Andreas fault: a major North American earthquake zone, which runs through California. San Francisco is on this fault line and suffered a serious earthquake in 1906

Jezebels: licentious women; from the biblical story of King Ahab's heathen wife in 1 Kings 21:15. Her name appears in the Apocalypse, denoting fanaticism and profligacy (Revelations 2:20)

I will greatly multiply thy sorrow: a reference to women's suffering in childbirth as God's punishment to Eve; see the Bible, Genesis 3:16

Agent Orange: a chemical defoliant used in Vietnam by the US

Airforce to remove ground cover protecting the
Viet Cong, and alleged to have damaging long-
term effects on humans

Chapter 20

Inside the house of Ofwarren's Commander, Offred's mind slips
away from the grotesquely theatrical natural childbirth performance,
as she remembers the Red Centre's brainwashing programmes with
their films about late twentieth-century cultural history and the position of women. In their combination of pornography and feminist
protest, they present an interesting, if biased, survey of sexual politics of the 1970s and 80s. In one of the films Offred with a shock
recognises her own mother at one of the feminist rallies about pornography and abortion in the 1970s, and she thinks back to her
mother's staunch feminist stance as a single parent, wishing that she
could have those days of comparative freedom back again.

NOTES AND GLOSSARY:
Birthing Stool: an old custom revived from Puritan New
England. It is described in Perry Miller's account
of seventeenth-century New England history (see
above, p. 13)
From each according to her ability: not a quotation from the Bible as
the women here are told; it actually stems from
a statement on capitalist methods of production
made by Karl Marx (1818–83)
TAKE BACK THE NIGHT: an anti-pornography slogan of American feminists in the 1970s
FREEDOM TO CHOOSE: a pro-abortion rights slogan from the same
period

Chapter 21

Back in the present at the birth, Offred notices the heat and the
female smells around her of sweat and blood as she chats with the
other Handmaids. When the baby is born, attention immediately
switches to the Wife who will rear the child, for Janine's duty as a
surrogate mother is now done. Thinking back to her own mother,
Offred realises how the feminist phrase 'a women's culture' has
been appropriated by conservative ideology in ways her mother's
generation would never have dreamed of. It is an example of the
Orwellian abuses of language which characterise the official rhetoric
of Gilead.

NOTES AND GLOSSARY:
matrix: uterus or womb (from Latin *mater*, mother)

Chapter 22

Returning home exhausted in the late afternoon, Offred tries to raise her spirits by remembering Moira's greatest act of rebellion, when she escaped from the Red Centre by tying up one of the Aunts in the basement and putting on her clothes. As an act of defiance, Moira's escape is wildly exciting to the others, but it is also frightening. Offred clearly recognises the dangers of an absolute system of control where people quickly get used to seeing themselves as victims and begin to lose the taste for freedom.

Chapter 23

There is a strong element of narrative surprise in this chapter, which begins with another of Offred's comments on her story-telling and why it is that no story can ever recapture the whole truth of human experience. She also makes a significant comment about different kinds of power, clearly distinguishing between tyranny and the power of love and forgiveness. This is the chapter in which she has her first secret meeting with the Commander in his study, and it represents a radical departure from the formality of their prescribed relationship. Well aware that it is illegal and dangerous, yet unable to refuse, she is surprised to find that when she walks into the forbidden room she walks back into what used to be normal life. The Commander's request is a strange one in the circumstances: all he wants is that Offred should play Scrabble with him, which she does. In the game she spells out words which refer to her own situation as a Handmaid, revelling in the forbidden privilege of playing games with words. She finds herself feeling sorry for the Commander who, she realises, is as isolated as she is herself.

NOTES AND GLOSSARY:
Larynx:	voice box
Valance:	bed canopy
Quince:	yellow pear-shaped fruit which has quite a bitter taste
Zygote:	fertilised cell, formed by the union of sperm and egg
Gorge:	throat (noun), and to eat gluttonously (verb)

Section 9. Chapter 24

Returning to her room, Offred thinks about her changed relationship with the Commander. With a newly awakened sense of her individuality, her mood is much lighter, and this short chapter ends with Offred's outburst of hysterical laughter. However, her situation is too precarious for her to feel carefree. She realises that she may be tempted into friendship with the Commander and remembers a television documentary about a Nazi war criminal's mistress who refused to believe that the man she loved was a monster. Of course Offred knows that she cannot laugh out loud at the absurdity of her situation, so she goes into the one hidden place in her room, into the cupboard where the secret message is scrawled, and there she laughs her defiance. The chapter ends with the word 'opening', for this is the signal of the end of Offred's traumatised condition and her opening out to life again.

NOTES AND GLOSSARY:

Liebchen: (*German*) dear, love

Hysteria: disorder of the nervous system to which women were thought to be more liable than men. The Elizabethans thought it was caused by a disturbance of the uterus

Section 10. Chapter 25

This chapter opens dramatically with 'a scream and a crash', for Offred has fallen asleep in the cupboard and Cora, the servant bringing her breakfast, thinks that Offred has killed herself like her predecessor. Offred, however, is more alive than at any point so far in the novel. High summer has come and she walks in the garden, dazzled by its beauty and giddy with desire in the midst of a pagan earthly paradise which celebrates the fecundity of nature denied by Gilead.

Indoors she is beginning to enjoy her illicit evenings in the Commander's study, where they play endless Scrabble games and he allows her to read his collection of out-of-date women's magazines (such as *Vogue* and *Ms*) while he sits watching her. Their activities would seem ordinary enough, but in Gilead they represent a breaking of taboos and a transgression of its prescribed pattern of male-female relations. She and the Commander establish something close to an intimate relationship on very traditional lines of the eternal triangle of husband, wife and mistress. This is a pattern that is both confirmed and questioned when Offred asks him to get her some hand lotion, which he does. She then realises that she has nowhere to keep it, so she has to use it in the Commander's study, and he watches her putting on the lotion with all the hungry pleasure of a voyeur.

NOTES AND GLOSSARY:

A Tennyson garden . . . swoon: 'swoon', meaning 'to faint', occurs in the poem 'The Lotos-Eaters' (1842) by Alfred Lord Tennyson, though the garden reference points to his poem 'Maud' (1855)

Prolix: wordy, tedious, long-winded

quartz: granular rock

quandary: dilemma

sylph: a spirit supposed to inhabit the air; also applied to a slender, graceful woman

Chapter 26

In this chapter Offred becomes aware of the dangers of her friendship with the Commander when the time comes around for the monthly Ceremony. She is now emotionally involved, and this inevitably complicates her relationship both with him and his Wife, for she now also takes the role of his mistress, not merely that of his Handmaid.

Chapter 27

Another new perspective opens up for Offred as she goes on her shopping expedition with Ofglen. Having passed the church and the Wall and the former university library, now the headquarters of the secret police, they go to stand outside 'Soul Scrolls', the computerised prayer factory. Here as they stare at each other's reflections in the shatterproof windows, Ofglen asks a surprising question which amounts to treason in Gilead, 'Do you think God listens to these machines?' When Offred answers 'No', they both confess that they are unbelievers, and Offred discovers that Ofglen is a member of the underground Mayday resistance group. This revelation gives Offred a surge of new hope and a sense of life and hope returning as they walk back in the sunshine.

The chapter ends, however, with a sharp reminder of the power of the regime they are up against, for as they walk along they see a man being brutally beaten up by the secret police in the street and nobody dares to take any notice. Offred realises the limits of her courage when she admits to herself that she is glad she is not the victim.

NOTES AND GLOSSARY:
Loaves and Fishes: for a description of Christ's miracle of the loaves
and fishes, see the Bible, Mark 6:38–44
Tibetan prayer wheels: cylindrical boxes inscribed with prayers,
revolving on a spindle; used especially by the
Buddhists of Tibet

Chapter 28

Offred thinks about her relationship with the Commander, and,
trying to see it as Moira might have done, she realises that there are
parallels to her early relation with Luke, for that too was an eternal
triangle situation: she was his mistress before she was his wife. She
moves from thinking about their married life to remembering her
job as a librarian and how she lost it. She then recalls how the
Gileadean regime came to power by a violent *coup d'état* and pro-
ceeded to implement its policies by stripping citizens of their political
and legal rights. Its social policies were specifically directed against
women, and married women were forcibly removed from the labour
market and returned to the home in Gilead's effort to bolster the
family structure for the moral good of society. What Offred remembers most clearly is her own state of shock and the way people were
too afraid to protest much. She also recalls her own resentment at
the loss of her economic freedom and her irrational anger against
Luke for still having a job when hers has been taken away from her.

In a switchback to the present, Offred sees Nick's signal that she
is to meet the Commander again and wonders what Nick thinks of
the arrangement.

NOTES AND GLOSSARY:
The Book of Job: this Old Testament story, like Offred's tale, is a
series of catastrophes recounted by the survivors
In God We Trust: motto on the American dollar bill

Chapter 29

In the Commander's study Offred now feels at ease playing Scrabble
and reading voraciously, and on this visit she dares to ask him the
meaning of the message in her cupboard. When he explains that it
is a schoolboy Latin joke meaning 'Don't let the bastards grind you
down', she realises that her predecessor must have learnt it from the
Commander too and that probably her predecessor's relationship
with him had been similar to her own. When he asks Offred if she
would like something as a kind of payment for her time spent with

him, she reveals her desire for some factual knowledge beyond the censored newscasts when she says that above all she would like to know what is going on in Gilead.

NOTES AND GLOSSARY:

Pen Is Envy: Red Centre motto based on Freudian psychoanalytic theory which presents 'penis envy' as an essential element of femininity, and a mark of women's natural inferiority to men

Venus de Milo: a famous, now armless, statue of the goddess of love, dating from the second century BC, which is to be found in the Louvre, Paris

Section 11. Chapter 30

It is night again, and Offred, while gazing out of her window, happens to see Nick. Remembering their encounter in the dark sitting-room, she feels the same sexual excitement and sense of frustration when a look of romantic longing is exchanged between them. Her mind flicks back from Nick to Luke and their failed escape attempt, and she realises that Luke and her daughter are beginning to seem like fading ghosts.

The chapter ends with Offred's saying the Lord's Prayer in her own ironic version, deliberately confusing the literal and symbolic meanings of the words as she tries to formulate her own position. Finally she gives way to a cry of despair at her own isolation and imprisonment and her fading hopes of release.

NOTES AND GLOSSARY:

Context is all; or is it ripeness?: compare with the line that appears in Shakespeare's *King Lear*, Act V, Scene 2: 'Ripeness is all'

Section 12. Chapter 31

This section contains Offred's account of her night out with the Commander at Jezebel's, a high-class brothel in Gilead. The section also includes many other examples of women's exploitation by, and resistance to, the regime.

In this chapter life goes on much as usual for Offred as she moves discreetly between her room and her shopping expeditions with Ofglen. Yet beneath the rules there are signs of women's resistance – not only Ofglen's secret network, but also Serena Joy's surprising offer. One day she calls Offred to her in the garden and actually suggests that she make an arrangement for Offred to sleep with Nick in order to conceive a child without the Commander's knowledge. Offred knows she is being used, but she also recognises that Wife and Handmaid have become conspirators working in secret together to subvert Gilead's rules. To seal the bargain, Serena gives Offred an illegal cigarette and offers to let her see at last a photograph of her lost daughter.

NOTES AND GLOSSARY:

Torahs: In Judaism the Torah is the sacred parchment scroll on which is written the Pentateuch (first five books of the Old Testament). It is preserved in all synagogues inside the Ark of the Law, and readings from the Torah form an important part of Jewish liturgical services

talliths: rectangular prayer shawls worn by male Jews during services

Mogen Davids: the star of David, composed of two equilateral overlapping triangles which form a six-pointed star. It appears on synagogues, Jewish tombstones and the Israeli flag

Chapter 32

In her room, Offred does not smoke the cigarette but hoards it and the match, and sits thinking about her relationship with the Commander. However, she has no doubt about her own powerlessness. When she lies down on her bed she feels more afraid than ever as she stares up at the blank space where the light fitting used to be. Now she knows why the space is blank: it was from that fitting that her predecessor hanged herself.

Chapter 33

Offred is taken on another of the Handmaids' compulsory outings, this time to a Prayvaganza, which is a Hollywood-style extravaganza and prayer meeting to celebrate a mass wedding. This regimented affair is one of the few entertainments for women, and Offred describes it as being like a circus or a theatrical performance. Amid this public rejoicing, Offred thinks of Janine as one of the casualties of the new system. She has just been told that Janine's baby girl was destroyed because she was deformed, and she remembers Janine almost having a nervous breakdown at the Red Centre, from which Moira saved her.

NOTES AND GLOSSARY:
Do you like butter?: a children's game played with buttercups held under the chin
Blow, and you tell the time: a children's game played by puffing at dandelions gone to seed
daisies for love: another game, played by pulling the petals off daisies and counting them to the words 'He loves me, he loves me not'

Chapter 34

The Prayvaganza focuses on Gilead's New Right ideology as spelled out to Offred by the Commander, according to which traditional male domination over women is justified as God's law and Nature's norm. In Gilead woman is defined by her biological destiny, and romantic love is dismissed as a brief ripple in the history of the human race. The arranged mass marriages between soldiers and daughters of Gileadean officials provide the occasion for laying down the law on woman's subjection and silence, which is endorsed by quotations from the Bible. But the irreverent comments by Offred and Ofglen suggest a general scepticism towards this doctrine.

NOTES AND GLOSSARY:
'There is a Balm in Gilead': an American folk hymn, the opening words of which are: 'There is a balm in Gilead to make the wounded whole / There is a balm in Gilead to heal the sinsick soul.' It is based on the Old Testament prophet Jeremiah's question, 'Is there no balm in Gilead; is there no physician there?' (Jeremiah 8:22)
mooning and June-ing: traditional romantic references which occur frequently in popular songs, for example, 'By the Light of the Silvery Moon' contains the words, 'Honeymoon, / keep a-shining in June'. This song, first used in the Ziegfeld Follies in 1909, was popular until the 1950s
'I will that women adorn themselves in modest apparel': see the Bible, 1 Timothy 2:9–15

Chapter 35

Back in her room again, Offred fills her blank time by thinking of the one element that the Prayvaganza left out of the marriage service: love. She has a long nostalgic digression on 'falling in love' which she is old enough to remember having done herself, for Offred is continually seeing the present through her memories of the past and judging it according to former values.

Her reverie is interrupted by Serena Joy, who appears with the photograph of Offred's daughter. For Offred, however, this is a new source of grief, since she thinks that she will have been forgotten by her daughter, just as she will be forgotten when the history of Gilead is written.

NOTES AND GLOSSARY:

That word, made flesh: see the Bible, John 1:14

White Russian drinking tea in Paris: aristocratic refugees from the Russian Revolution in 1917 went into exile throughout Europe and there were a large number of them in Paris in the 1920s. They were known as 'white Russians' because they opposed the Red Army of the Bolsheviks

Chapter 36

The Commander breaks all the rules by inviting Offred to dress up and go out with him one evening. It is a bizarre enterprise as well as a dangerous one, but Offred accepts, partly because she cannot refuse and partly because she craves some excitement. The Commander produces an old purple satin costume with feathers and sequins plus high-heeled shoes, and he even supplies the make-up and a mirror and a cloak which he has borrowed secretly from his Wife – an irony not lost upon Offred.

It is Nick who has to drive them on this clandestine outing, but Offred cannot tell what he is thinking. As they drive down a back alley and hurry through a dark entrance, Offred is left in no doubt of the Commander's attitude, for he ties a label on her wrist and steers her in as if she were an object which he has won or perhaps just rented for the evening.

Chapter 37

'Jezebel's' is an episode which is both comic and bleak. The place to which the Commander takes Offred is familiar to her because it turns out to be the hotel where she had formerly come with Luke during their affair, but the scenario is oddly unfamiliar, for it is like a film, not real life.

Forbidden under Gilead's Puritanical rules, the place is nevertheless maintained as a state-run brothel for officers and foreign trade delegations, and what it represents are pornographic male fantasies about women. There are women dressed up in baby-doll pyjamas or Bunny Girl costumes, also some dressed like devils and *femmes fatales*; everything is entirely focused on male fantasy and desire. These women are here because they refused to be assimilated as Handmaids, and their only alternative to being sent to the Colonies was to join the staff at the brothel. They are 'professionals' (both in the sense of professional career women and in the sense of prostitutes) and dissidents, but officially they do not exist.

Offred suddenly sees Moira, in an outfit even more grotesque than her own. By their old secret signal they agree to meet in the women's washroom, and Offred excuses herself from the Commander, leaving him sipping his drink in the lounge.

Chapter 38

In the washroom, presided over by an Aunt disguised as a Madame, Offred and Moira manage to tell each other what has happened to them since Moira's escape from the Red Centre. Of course it is Moira who suggests that the Commander brought Offred to Jezebel's as part of a male power fantasy, and there is plenty of evidence for this feminist analysis.

Offred embeds the story of Moira's escape attempt inside her own narrative, partly to celebrate Moira's heroism and that of all the people who helped her get as far as the Canadian border, but partly as an elegy to Moira whom Offred will never see again after tonight. The sad truth is that Moira has not managed to escape from Gilead any more than Offred's unknown predecessor; the most that Offred can do if she survives is to tell their stories of resistance.

NOTES AND GLOSSARY:

Whore of Babylon: a joking reference to the wicked scarlet woman depicted in the Apocalypse; see the Bible, Revelation 17:3–5

Underground Femaleroad: an allusion to the Underground Railroad, which was an escape route for runaway slaves from the United States to Canada between 1840 and 1860, prior to the abolition of slavery after the American Civil War. It was an informal network of safe houses and people. About 30,000 slaves reached Canada that way, and the last former slave died in Ontario in 1971

Chapter 39

In this chapter the Commander takes Offred upstairs for what he assumes will be a pleasurable sexual encounter for them both, but it is doomed to be a failure. A private relationship between Offred and the Commander is not possible, for the personal has become inescapably political. There are too many memories of Luke in the hotel, and Offred also remembers Moira's account of her mother being sent to the Colonies by the Gileadean regime. Offred cannot forget that the Commander represents the tyrannical power of Gilead which is responsible for her losses and that she is his slave. Consequently she does not want to see him as a naked human being without his uniform on, and would prefer the grotesque relationship with Serena Joy present as well. In bed she feels she has to pretend to enjoy it, both for the Commander's sake and for her own safety, but the encounter is a dismal failure.

NOTES AND GLOSSARY:

I'll turn into a pumpkin: a reference to the Cinderella fairy-tale, where at the stroke of midnight the heroine is changed back from a princess to a kitchen maid, the coach is turned back into a pumpkin and the footmen back into mice

Section 13. Chapter 40

By contrast to the last chapter, this one describes Offred's romantic love affair with Nick. Although she knows she is still being used, this time by the Commander's Wife, her encounter with Nick is entirely different and her account of their first love-making is curiously reticent about what really happened. She tries to tell it in three different ways, but she admits that none of them is true because no language can adequately describe the complex experience of falling in love. In this precarious situation there is for Offred the further problem of her infidelity to Luke and her ignorance about his fate, all of which is part of the dilemma of human love explored by Offred in her narrative.

Section 14. Chapter 41

Perhaps to underline the precariousness of her illicit love affair with Nick, Offred embeds it in this most gruesome section of the novel, in which she describes a public execution and an outbreak of mob violence.

Offred begins by speculating once more on the function of her narrative, which works both as an eye-witness account and as a substitute for dialogue. Addressing her imaginary reader, she warns that this next part of her story does no credit to her, but she is determined to try to tell the truth as she feels that her reader deserves it. The love scenes with Nick are both ambiguous and tender. Offred is totally compromised not only in relation to her memories of Luke, but in her official relation with the Commander and her unofficial relation with Ofglen's resistance movement. She is also in danger of being shot by mistake in the dark. Yet to her, being in love again is like a refuge in the wilderness, and she abandons herself to the feeling, celebrating this crucial human emotion which Gileadean tyranny cannot wipe out. For the first time she actually wants to stay in Gilead, as long as she can be with Nick.

NOTES AND GLOSSARY:

Salvaging: the word has associations with 'salvage,' 'salvation' and 'savage'. Elsewhere Margaret Atwood has commented that in the Philippines salvaging has now come to mean 'public execution', a startling example of the abuse of language

'I tell, therefore you are': a punning variation of René Descartes' '*Cogito ergo sum*' ('I think, therefore I am') from his *Discourse on Method* (1637), where he defines thought as the essential characteristic of a human being. Atwood's version emphasises language and communication rather than the self-enclosed mind

Chapter 42

The Salvaging is another compulsory outing, this time to witness the execution of two Handmaids and one Wife. Again it is a showbiz event, set outdoors on the lawn in front of what was once the university library, and it reminds Offred of a graduation ceremony until the proceedings begin. It is not, however, even a show trial, for the women are hanged for unspecified crimes. It is a frightening display of fanaticism presided over by Aunt Lydia in which all Handmaids are forced to become collaborators, for they all have to put their hands on the hanging rope to signify their assent to these killings.

Chapter 43

The Salvaging reaches a horrendous climax in the public slaughter of a man supposed to have been convicted of rape. This 'Particicution' is a dreadful spectacle of female violence, for it is the Handmaids who are encouraged to kill and dismember him. It is conducted by Aunt Lydia who blows a whistle as in a football game. Everyone is overcome by a wave of hysteria and revenge, though Offred notices that the man tries to smile and to deny the charge. Ofglen rushes forward and kicks the man to knock him out, and the chapter ends with Ofglen telling Offred that the man was not a rapist but a member of the resistance movement. Then Janine appears with a smear of blood across her cheek as she drifts away into madness. Offred's own reaction makes her extremely uncomfortable, for the man's terrible death has acted on her like a stimulant, enhancing her own sense of physical survival.

NOTES AND GLOSSARY:

a kind of dance: this recalls the film *The Red Shoes* (1948), starring Moira Shearer as the ballerina who danced herself to death

Particicution: the word contains 'participation' (by the Handmaids) and 'execution' (of the victim)

Deuteronomy 22:23–29: Gilead follows the Old Testament law that the penalty for rape is death

Chapter 44

Later that same afternoon when Offred goes shopping, thinking that things have returned to what is normal in Gilead, she is astonished to find that she has a different partner and her friend Ofglen has been replaced by someone else (who is now 'Ofglen'). Again Offred feels the threat of risk but cannot contain her curiosity about her friend. She is even more astonished to be told that the former Ofglen hanged herself after the Salvaging because she saw the black van coming for her.

Chapter 45

The knowledge that Ofglen committed suicide before she could be made to confess and endanger her friends in the resistance brings Offred to her worst crisis of despair. She finds that she is prepared to accept survival at any price and feels for the first time that she has been defeated and overpowered by Gilead. This is also the moment when Serena Joy confronts her with a more personal betrayal, holding out the cloak and the purple costume as evidence of her evening out with the Commander. She also tells Offred that what she did was what her predecessor had done, and that she will meet the same fate. Offred can do nothing except go up to her room alone.

Section 15. Chapter 46

This last chapter is very dramatic, both in the sense of being like a play with Offred as the character centre stage, and in terms of the surprise twist of the ending. It begins with Offred sitting in her room in a state of torpid indifference while she considers a variety of possible escapes, but does nothing. This is her moment of total despair when she feels as trapped as her predecessor, whose defiance ended in suicide.

Then comes a break in the text and an astonishing intervention, for suddenly Offred hears the siren of the black van and a group of Eyes led by Nick push open her door. Offred fears that Nick has betrayed her, but he whispers that he represents her only chance to escape, and she has no alternative but to believe him and go with the Eyes.

So Offred departs from the Commander's house, escorted out like a criminal and ridden with guilt at having let down everyone in the household, who all stand gaping at her in disbelief. Offred has no idea whether she is about to go to prison or to freedom, but she allows herself to be helped up into the van and she also allows herself to hope as she makes her exit. In the midst of her uncertainty and powerlessness it is a final gesture of trust and faith.

Historical Notes

These Notes are a supplement to the story we have just finished reading and they provide a framework for looking back at Offred's narrative from a distant point in the future when Gilead is in ruins and all the protagonists of the story are dead. It is also a view from outside the United States, for this conference paper is being given in Arctic Canada by a male archivist from the University of Cambridge, England. The session is chaired by a woman professor whose name suggests that she is a member of the Native peoples, who are now evidently in charge of their own educational policies.

As well as providing necessary background information, the Notes tell us how Offred's story has survived. It was not written down but recorded on cassette tapes which were unearthed on the site of the ruined city of Bangor, Maine. It is a transcription of these tapes, discovered and edited by two Cambridge professors, which we have been reading.

The Notes alter our perspective on Offred, for here she is no longer a living, suffering human being but an elusive anonymous voice whose story is nothing more than an anecdote in ancient history. As readers we may well object to this distancing technique, which is as reductive of Offred's identity as Gilead's depersonalising of her as one of its Handmaids. Professor Pieixoto cannot identify Offred, partly because her real name was already obscured by the Gileadean patronymic and partly because he spends most of his time trying to identify her Commander whose name was probably a pseudonym. He is really much more interested in pursuing an 'objective' view of history and in analysing Gileadean social theory in a broadly historical context. For all his scholarship he cannot get beyond generalities and fails to tell us what we most want to know, that is, what happened to Offred. We are likely to feel that his historical interpretation misses the point, and that, ironically, his only useful role is as a male Handmaid who has succeeded in bringing Offred's tale to light. We may be thankful for his scholarly endeavours, as, through them, her tale has survived, but now that it is available Offred can at last speak for herself.

The final question invites us as readers to participate in interpreting the multiple and contradictory meanings of what we have just finished reading.

NOTES AND GLOSSARY:

University of Denay, Nunavit: these place names are significant. The Dene are Native people who live in northern Alberta, Canada. Nunavut is the name of a large area of the North West Territories in Canada, which is set to become a self-governing area by and for the Inuit people (formerly known as Eskimos). 'Denay, Nunavit' is also a pun on 'Deny none of it', referring to the story Offred has told us. We are advised to believe her story, whatever interpretations or misinterpretations might be offered in the 'Historical Notes'

Krishna and Kali elements: a reference to Hindu mythology; in Hinduism Krishna is the most benign of the gods and Kali is the ferocious goddess of death and destruction

Sumptuary Laws: laws regulating expenditure, especially with a view to restraining excess spending on food or equipment

Monotheocracies: systems of absolute government supported by the doctrine that there is only one God

Arctic Char: a salmon-like fish found in the North West Territories, which is an important source of food and income for the Inuits

enjoy: the 'obsolete third' sense of the word is 'to have sexual relations with a woman'

soi-disant: (*French*) so-called

Geoffrey Chaucer: Chaucer's *The Canterbury Tales* (*c*.1387) includes two women's tales, the 'Wife of Bath's Tale' and the 'Prioress's Tale', one emphasising sexual love and the other spiritual love

tail: the pun refers to the American slang expression for woman reduced to her sexual function, for example, 'a nice bit of tail'

'Elvis Presley's Golden Years': an album of the American rock and roll singer Elvis Presley's (1935–77) best songs, recorded in 1964. The songs, however, belong to the period 1956–8

'Folk Songs from Lithuania': an example of mid-1980s 'Roots Revolution' ethnic songs

'Boy George Takes It Off': a deliberately provocative album by the British pop singer, George O'Dowd (*b*.1961), made in the mid-1980s

'Mantovani's Mellow Strings': Mantovani's orchestral music was popular in the early 1960s, and this recording was made in 1961

'Twisted Sister at Carnegie Hall': a tape of a live show by this mid-1980s Californian rock group, whose male lead singer dressed in women's clothes

Darwinism: Charles Darwin's *The Origin of Species* (1859) puts forward the theory of natural selection and 'descent with modification' among species, and it contains the concept of the 'survival of the fittest'

Aunts should take names derived from commercial products: for example, Aunt Elizabeth (Elizabeth Arden cosmetics), Aunt Sara (Sara Lee cakes), Aunt Helena (Helena Rubinstein cosmetics)

Byzantine: extremely complicated, referring to the complexity of the administrative system developed in Byzantium, or Constantinople, the eastern division of the Roman Empire, which remained in existence from the fourth to the fifteenth centuries

Eurydice: a reference to Greek mythology. Eurydice was
the wife of Orpheus who rescued her from the
dead, but when he turned to look back at her
near the gates of Hades she was snatched back
into the Underworld and vanished for ever

Part 3

Commentary

Interpreting the text

The Handmaid's Tale is a novel about the future which is set uncomfortably close to our time in the present. Offred's first-person narrative is quite specific in its reference to one particular society at one particular historical moment, for this is her story of a nightmarish United States of America at the end of the twentieth century when democratic institutions have been violently overthrown and replaced by the new republic of Gilead, a police state run by religious fundamentalists. She tells of her life as a Handmaid in a period of violent transition from a Western society we are familiar with, to a different society which is Bible-based, socially repressive and totalitarian.

This invented world is at once familiar and unfamiliar, and is presented with such attention to documentary detail that it appears real. The narrator's urgent intention is to convince us that this is the way things are for her as a woman in Gilead. Yet we find at the end that she is already dead by the time we read her story and that Gilead has disappeared into ancient history. We never find out what happened to Offred after she escaped from the Commander's house, and so we are left with a sense of incompleteness. Moreover, the novel ends on a question, which we are invited to answer in our interpretation of the text.

As an open-ended novel it encourages an open-ended reading, though this raises the question of how free we are to make our own interpretations. Of course this does not mean that there ought to be only one possible reading, but at the same time there are guidelines suggested by the text and warnings against misreadings. After all, we have a terrifying example of misreading in the novel itself, in Gilead's interpretation of the Old Testament. We would all probably agree that this interpretation is fatally flawed when we see it in practice. Then there is the interpretation of Offred's story offered by Professor Pieixoto in the 'Historical Notes'. His is a scholarly editor's reading of an ancient document (transcribed by him from old cassette tapes) and we may well feel that his interpretation leaves out the crucial element of the Handmaid's tale: the personality and private resistance campaign of Offred herself. The novel demonstrates that wrong or inadequate interpretations of texts are possible.

What guidance, then, is there for us as readers from within the novel? For a start, the prefatory material gives us some clues by pointing to the Puritan and Old Testament elements, the social satire, and the themes of ecology and human survival which will be so important in the tale. The 'Historical Notes' insist that Offred's story and Gilead's story are both finished. Then the final question opens up the debate again, inviting us to be participants in the interpretative process.

The text may be read in at least four ways, depending on which features we choose to highlight. It may be read as anti-utopian fiction, as feminist fiction, as fictive autobiography, or as a love story.

There is plenty of evidence for reading it as an anti-utopian vision of a totalitarian future in Offred's account of daily life in Gilead, with its violence and bloodshed, its petty persecutions, and its denial of any rights of privacy or individuality. (One mark of this is its suppression of individual names, for everyone is given a classification name only, for example, Offred the Handmaid of Fred.) Gilead also provides one version of a future world polluted and with a catastrophically low birthrate, run by a political tyranny rationalised as the only way of saving the human race. The social organisation of Gilead also provides a satiric commentary on current trends in Western society and a warning against continuing unchecked movement in the direction in which our own technological society is going.

The Handmaid's Tale is also a feminist anti-utopian novel cast in the form of a prison narrative, for Offred is a virtual prisoner in the Commander's house. Gilead's exclusive focus on woman's biological role has led to a social redefinition of feminine identity in these terms alone. Women are classified as breeders and non-breeders. The state has developed an elaborate social policy to change women's ways of thinking about themselves. (What else could be the function of the Rachel and Leah Re-education Centre?) The novel also analyses the different strands of thought within late twentieth-century feminism, exposing some of its blind spots and contradictions. Yet this is an analysis produced by Atwood's own feminist awareness of gender-based power structures and women's traditionally vulnerable position in political, legal and economic terms. The collaboration of the Aunts in the male power game also raises the question: Has feminism gone far enough? Has it changed women's attitudes sufficiently for them to withstand male pressure at a time of national crisis? Offred's narrative of private resistance presents a 'feminine' alternative to the belief in male mastery, for she offers the values of love, hope and forgiveness, values which are marginalised by Gilead as unimportant. Yet it is her story which survives when Gilead's own records have been destroyed.

At the centre of the novel is Offred's autobiographical account.

She tells us about her life in a society which is governed by strict rules for public and private life. Its legal code is the Law of the Father – that of God and his agents, who are the bureaucrats. Interestingly, there are no ministers of religion here; priests are executed and so are Quakers, for this is a secular government run by Commanders, Eyes, Guardians, Angels and Aunts. It is the absolute rule of Gilead that Offred is always resisting, testing its limits, finding its weak points, motivated as she is by outdated concepts of individualism and freedom of choice, and valuing all the social and psychological variations of human beings which run counter to any fixed system of arbitrary rules. Her resistance lies in her refusal to be bound by these rules. She refuses to forget the past; she refuses to forget her own name as the sign of her buried identity; she refuses to give up hope of a different future. In fact she refuses to be trapped in the present, for she is continually slipping away from it in memory or imagination. Her principal activity of story-telling invents listeners and allows her to imagine a world beyond Gilead.

She insists on telling the stories of other silenced women which contradict Gilead's claims to absolute mastery and its myth of female submissiveness. From a wide historical perspective, she can be seen as writing against the Old Testament dismissal of the Handmaids of the Patriarchs, and she is writing on behalf of all those women then and now with no rights of representation. In this way her narrative is exemplary and symbolic. (It could even be compared with those eighteenth-century American slave narratives which Margaret Atwood recalls in her oblique reference to the 'Underground Railroad' for slaves escaping from the United States to Canada.)

The novel also tells a love story, or rather two love stories, one in the past, involving Offred's lost husband Luke, and one in the present, involving Nick the Commander's chauffeur. By focusing on powerful human feelings which Gilead neglects, Offred's story demonstrates that 'the human heart remains a factor' ('Historical Notes'). Love is the greatest challenge to the system's absolute authority, and finally love provides the very means for Offred's escape. We should not forget that Offred also tells the story of her sexual relationship with the Commander, which is certainly not a love story, though what kind of story it is she never quite manages to define.

All of the preceding elements need to be considered when interpreting *The Handmaid's Tale*. We are quite specifically reminded of this by the Author's injunction at the beginning of the 'Historical Notes', which is coded into the name of the place where the academic conference is being held: 'Denay, Nunavit' (Deny none of it).

Offred's narrative, though set in the future, is urgent and compelling in its immediacy; it also has international and historical resonances which stretch back to the Old Testament and forward into our own contemporary world.

Utopias and anti-utopias

The tradition of utopian fiction in our Western culture goes back to the Ancient Greeks with Plato's *Republic*, written about 350BC. Writers have always invented imaginary good societies (utopias) and imaginary bad societies (anti-utopias or dystopias) in order to comment on distinctive features and trends of their own societies. Utopias and anti-utopias are not merely fantasy worlds, but, as Krishan Kumar describes them in his book *Utopianism* (1991), they are imaginary places 'and accordingly futile to seek out, that nevertheless exist tantalisingly [or frighteningly] on the edge of possibility, somewhere just beyond the boundary of the real' (p.1). These fictions always have a kind of mirror relation to the writer's own world. They may offer models for the future, or more frequently they may make satiric attacks on present society and deliver strong warnings against the consequences of particular kinds of political and social behaviour.

Margaret Atwood said in a review of Marge Piercy's *Woman on the Edge of Time* (1976), 'Utopias are products of the moral rather than the literary sense', and as political or social commentary they have a strongly didactic element. They need to be read with some knowledge of the context of their own time to enable the reader to see the particularities of the society in which they were produced. Sir Thomas More's *Utopia* (published in Latin in 1516 and translated into English in 1551) is concerned with the possibilities for a better society that were being opened up by the discovery of the New World of America, whereas nearly five hundred years later *The Handmaid's Tale* is warning against threats of environmental pollution and religious fundamentalism in that same New World which has become the United States of America.

Margaret Atwood's negative vision of tyranny, women's enslavement and ecological disaster belongs to a long line of anti-utopian fictions which goes back to Jonathan Swift's *Gulliver's Travels* (1726) and includes some remarkable twentieth-century novels such as Aldous Huxley's *Brave New World* (1932) and George Orwell's *Nineteen Eighty-Four* (1949). Women have also written utopian and anti-utopian fictions, or, more frequently, fictions that mix the two. Charlotte Perkins Gilman's *Herland* (1915) is about a gently pastoral matriarchal society in the jungle, whose existence is threatened when men enter it, while Ursula Le Guin's *The Dispossessed* (1974), Marge Piercy's *Woman on the Edge of Time* and Joanna Russ's *The Female Man* (1975) all combine negative social criticism with visions of a better future.

The Handmaid's Tale is unambiguously anti-utopian fiction in its exposure of power politics in a male-dominated world where women and nature are relentlessly exploited as 'national resources'. Atwood's Gilead is her strong warning against the policies and assumptions of late twentieth-century Western technological society, told from the woman's point of view. As she also makes plain in the 'Historical Notes', Gilead turns out to have been an unworkable social experiment. As she said in an interview in 1987, 'I'm an optimist. I like to show that the Third Reich, the Fourth Reich, the Fifth Reich did not last forever',* and she compares her 'Historical Notes' with Orwell's note on Newspeak at the end of *Nineteen Eighty-Four*.

Many of the themes of *The Handmaid's Tale* are to be found in *Nineteen Eighty-Four*. It offers a similar warning against threats of totalitarianism in the not too distant future, and delineates the ways in which any totalitarian state tries to control not only the lives but also the thoughts of its subjects. There are similar efforts to silence opposition at any price, and both novels warn against the dangers of propaganda and censorship. Atwood pays particular attention to the abuses of language in Gilead where the meanings of words are changed to their opposites, as in Orwell's Newspeak, in an effort to restructure the way people are allowed to think about their world. For example, the Gileadean rhetoric of 'Aunts', 'Angels', 'Salvagings' takes words with reassuring emotional connotations and distorts them into euphemisms for the instruments of oppression. There is, however, one major difference between *The Handmaid's Tale* and *Nineteen Eighty-Four*: Atwood's novel is told from the point of view of an 'ignorant peripherally involved woman'. (Incidentally, this is the same point of view that she adopted in her previous novel, *Bodily Harm*.) Offred is not Orwell's Winston Smith and she does not come to love Big Brother (or in her case, the Commander) in the end. Instead she escapes and tells her story as a narrative of resistance, for she is never persuaded into forgetting that there is another world and other, better values beyond Gilead.

The novel is set in the United States, because, as Atwood has said, 'The States are more extreme in everything . . . Everyone watches the States to see what the country is doing and might be doing ten or fifteen years from now'.† This is a futuristic scenario but close

Conversations, p. 223.
†*Conversations*, p. 217.

enough to our time, for the protagonist herself has grown up in the permissive society of the 1970s and 80s and is at the time of telling her story only thirty-three years old. Some of the features of Gilead could apply to any late twentieth-century state with advanced technology and pollution problems. It is, however, specifically an American location, as we learn not only from the 'Historical Notes', but also from details within Offred's narrative, as, for example, from the Gileadean take-over 'when they shot the President and machine-gunned the Congress' (Chapter 28), Moira's escape along Mass Avenue (Chapter 38), and July the Fourth, the former Independence Day (Chapter 31). The novelist herself signals the particular historical, social and political context in her 'What if' statement (see 'Introduction'). There is also a strong sense of American Puritan history here, establishing connections between seventeenth-century New England, with its Salem witch hunts, and late twentieth-century Gilead, with its New Right ideology and its religious fanaticism.

Not only is it a 'Back to the Future' scenario but it is also a period of crisis, for the novel deals with the new anti-utopian society at its moment of transition. Offred herself is facing both ways, but so is Gilead, with all its citizens and its leaders remembering the capitalist era and its culture. Gilead is a bizarre mixture of fundamentalist principles, late twentieth-century technology and a Hollywood-style propaganda machine. It also has history upon which to draw, for 'there was little that was truly original with or indigenous to Gilead: its genius was synthesis' ('Historical Notes').

We need, however, to remember that this is anti-utopian fiction told from the woman's point of view and that Offred does take liberties with the conventions of the genre. As the male professor complains in the 'Historical Notes', 'She could have told us much about the workings of the Gileadean empire, had she had the instincts of a reporter or a spy.' Offred does have these instincts, but she chooses to report not on public but on private matters. It is on the experiences of women in Gilead – Wives, Handmaids, Aunts, Daughters, Marthas, rebels and Unwomen – that she focuses her attention. She tells some of the little personal narratives that challenge the patriarchal narrative of Gilead, and ironically it is her tale which survives long after Gilead has fallen.

Narrative technique

The Handmaid's Tale is a woman's narrative that challenges the absolute authority of Gilead, highlighting the significance of story-telling as an act of resistance against oppression, thereby making a particular kind of individual political statement. We might approach

Offred's narrative through Atwood's own comments as a writer who is also an active member of Amnesty International:

> I'm an artist . . . and in any monolithic regime I would be shot. They *always* do that to artists. Why? Because the artists are messy. They don't fit. They make squawking noises. They protest. They insist on some kind of standard of humanity which any such regime is going to violate. They will violate it saying that it's for the good of all, or the good of the many, or the better this or better that. And the artists will always protest and they'll always get shot. Or go into exile.*

and

> The writer . . . retains three attributes that power-mad regimes cannot tolerate: a human imagination, in the many forms it may take, the power to communicate, and hope.†

These statements on the writer's role provide a gloss on Offred's position as teller of this tale, for she insists on voicing her own point of view when the regime demands total silence. But Offred's freedom is very circumscribed and she cannot tell her story within the Gileadean context. She can only tell it after she has escaped. We learn at the end that what we have read as her story is a reassembled transcript of a jumble of cassette recordings that have been found on an archaeological site. What we have is a later reconstruction of Offred's reconstruction told after her escape, and by the time of our reading Offred herself has disappeared. Yet story-telling is the only possible gesture against the silences of death and of history.

The emphasis throughout is on process and reconstruction, where 'truth' is only a matter of the teller's perspective, as Offred often reminds us. Her narrative is a discontinuous one, with its frequent time shifts, short scenes, and its unfinished ending. As Margaret Atwood said, in reply to an interviewer,

> [Offred] was boxed in. How do you tell a narrative from the point of view of that person? The more limited and boxed in you are, the more important details become . . . Details, episodes separate themselves from the flow of time in which they're embedded.**

Offred's story opens with her going to sleep in an unspecified detention camp which we later learn is the Rachel and Leah Re-education Centre for Handmaids. In the second chapter, still in the present time but at a point later than the first, she describes her

---

Conversations, p. 183.
†'Amnesty International: An Address', 1981, in *Second Words*, p. 397.
**Conversations*, p. 216.

room in a comfortably old-fashioned house where she is constrained
to follow a set routine and to wear a bizarre red uniform. It is not
until Chapter 3 that her situation becomes clearer, when in a flashback she tells how she arrived at the house to become a Handmaid.

Only gradually through flashbacks does she piece together how it
all happened, and it is this process of bringing together the present
and the past which constitutes the narrative interest and the psychological construction of Offred as a believable character. We come to
understand Offred's condition of double vision, for she continually
sees and judges the present through her memories of the past. As
she says, 'You'll have to forgive me. I'm a refugee from the past,
and like other refugees I go over the customs and habits of being
I've left or been forced to leave behind me' (Chapter 35).

Her flashes of memory tend to come as scenic units, unbidden and
incomplete during the day as disruptions of her routine, but sustained
at night, either in dreams or indulged in as an escape: 'But the night
is my time out. Where should I go? Somewhere good' (Chapter 7).
Through such flashes we learn the details of Offred's personal history
and the social history of Gilead. It is, of course, possible to set down
the chapters where flashbacks occur; thus, Offred's memories of her
relationship with Luke and their family life together are to be found
in Chapters 5, 12, 18, 28 and 39, and her recurrent nightmare of
their failed attempt to escape over the border to Canada appears in
Chapters 7, 13, 14, 30 and 35. The story of Gilead's take-over of the
US government appears as flashback in Chapter 28, and the social
effects of it on women are detailed in Chapter 38. What is most
noticeable is the discontinuous nature of these episodes and also the
ways in which they are frequently connected with crises in Offred's
present life. The narrative represents the complex ways that memory
works, where the present moment is never self-contained but per-
vaded by traces of other times and events.

Offred is not fixed in the past; indeed she is also, like Pamela (in
Samuel Richardson's epistolary novel *Pamela*, published in 1742),
writing of the present, and her record of her daily life is presented
with scrupulous attention to realistic detail. She records the unexcit-
ing monotony of her daily life as a Handmaid, as well as its crises,
both public and personal. There are the public meetings like the
Birth Day, the Prayvaganza and the terrible Salvaging; there is also
of course the monthly Ceremony (which occurs two or three times
in the story); there are her own significant private events, like her
secret meetings with the Commander and their outing to Jezebel's
where she meets Moira again. However ambivalent are her feelings
for the Commander, Offred recognises that it is through these meetings in his study where she can talk and read that she is enabled to

return to a lively sense of herself as an individual. Most crucial for her is her love affair with Nick (Chapters 40 and 41), which has, as she recognises, all the conventional features of a romantic love story and possibly even a happy ending. Yet in the circumstances it is the most unlikely plot that could have been devised, and Offred tells it with a kind of dazzled disbelief in its reality.

Offred tells the stories of many other women as well as her own. Some of these are fixed in the past and some end even while she is telling her own. The story of her feminist mother belongs to the past and is recaptured only in memory and on film (Chapters 7 and 39). Moira's story, like her mother's, is one on which Offred draws for strength in her gallery of female heroism, but unlike her mother, Moira is not fixed in the pre-Gileadean past. Her story does start there, in their student days which Offred recalls in Chapter 7 and Chapter 10, but it has a sequel for she too becomes an inmate at the Rachel and Leah Centre, and Offred recalls with delight Moira's courage and outrageousness in Chapters 13, 15 and 22 when Moira escapes. Offred finds Moira again at Jezebel's in Chapter 37 and tells the story of her life as a rebel in Chapter 38. Hers is one of the unfinished stories embedded in this narrative, for Offred never sees Moira again after that night.

There are also shorter story fragments about other Handmaids, all of them rebels or victims or both, which form a sad subtext to Offred's story of survival and incidentally imply a moral judgment on the social engineering policies of Gilead. There is the story of her stubborn unnamed predecessor at the Commander's house, of whom all she knows is the scribbled secret message (Chapter 9) and scraps of information about how she hanged herself from the chandelier in her room (Chapter 29). For Offred, that woman is her own ghostly double: 'How could I have believed I was alone in here? There were always two of us. Get it over, she says' (Chapter 46).

The principle of doubling comes up again in the story of Ofglen, Offred's shopping partner: 'Doubled, I walk the street' (Chapter 5). Yet Ofglen turns out to be more like Moira's double than Offred's, for she too is a rebel in disguise, a member of the Mayday Resistance movement and a whisperer of irreverent comments at the Prayvaganza. But her story does have an ending, for she commits suicide after the Salvaging (Chapter 44).

Whether women are rebels or willing victims, their chances of survival are slim, as the story of Janine illustrates. She appears and reappears in Offred's story, marking the various stages of a Handmaid's career – from willing victim at the Rachel and Leah Centre where she almost has a nervous breakdown (Chapter 33), to her moment of triumph as the pregnant Ofwarren whose Birth Day is attended by all the Handmaids (Chapters 19 and 21), to her last frightening appearance as madwoman after the Particicution, holding a clump of bloodstained hair (Chapter 43).

Offred also tells the story of the Commander's Wife, with flash-backs to her earlier career as a television personality on a gospel show in Chapters 3 and 8, and much satiric detail of Serena Joy's behaviour in the present. Yet in a curious way, though it could not be seen as an example of female bonding, Offred's account presents Serena Joy as another of her own doubles – another woman trapped by Gileadean domestic ideology. In one of her odder anecdotes, Offred is even disguised as Serena Joy when she has to wear her blue cloak to go with the Commander to the forbidden Jezebel's, and she is forced to look at her own face in Serena Joy's silver mirror to put on her make-up on that occasion.

There is yet another dimension to Offred's complex narrative, which signals the very contemporary nature of Margaret Atwood's story-telling technique. Offred is continually drawing our attention to her story-telling process, commenting on the way that the act of telling shapes and changes real experience, and giving reasons why she needs to tell her story at all (see Chapters 7, 23, 40 and 41). For Offred, story-telling is both eye-witness account and substitute for dialogue. It is also the only message she can hope to send to the outside world from her imprisonment, and she has to struggle to tell it, trusting that one day her message will be delivered:

A story is like a letter. *Dear You*, I'll say. Just *you*, without a name. Attaching a name attaches *you* to the world of fact, which is riskier, more hazardous: who knows what the chances are out there, of survival, yours? I will say *you*, *you*, like an old love song. *You* can mean more than one.

You can mean thousands.

I'm not in any immediate danger, I'll say to you.

I'll pretend you can hear me.

But it's no good, because I know you can't.   (Chapter 7)

Offred's story ends when she climbs up into the black van, but the novel does not end here. There is a supplement in the 'Historical Notes', told by a different narrator, Professor Pieixoto. This shift in time perspective and point of view works paradoxically to convince us of the immediacy of Offred's narrative. It is very likely that we will reject the professor's dismissal of Offred as a figure belonging to the past, and given his own sexist attitudes towards her story and toward the Chairperson (who is a woman) we may also become convinced that Offred's story about patriarchal attitudes does not belong exclusively to the past but threatens the future as well. There is no answer to the final sentence: 'Are there any questions?' No doubt the learned Cambridge professor did overrun his time period, despite having been asked by Professor Maryann Crescent Moon to keep within it!

Characters

Offred

Offred is the narrator and the main protagonist of *The Handmaid's Tale*, for this is her story of resistance and survival within Gilead. When we first meet her (or rather, when we first hear her voice, for that is how we come to know her, through her narration) she is already trapped in Gilead at the Rachel and Leah Centre, and is about to become a Handmaid dressed in red. Offred is a Handmaid throughout her story, but she refuses to be confined by this definition and continually subverts the identity which has been imposed on her.

As a Handmaid she is deprived of her own name and citizenship, defined entirely in biological terms as a 'two-legged womb', whose body is at the service of the state. She is housed, clothed, fed and washed as a valuable national resource (like a 'prize pig', as she ironically describes herself) and reduced to a red shape, for 'blood defines us'. At the age of thirty-three and potentially still fertile, she is a victim of Gileadean sexist ideology which equates 'male' with power and sexual potency and 'female' with reproduction and submission to the point where individuality is effaced. Offred's narrative, however, does not possess such diagrammatic simplicity, for she resists such reductiveness by a variety of stratagems that allow her to retain a sense of her own individuality and psychological freedom in what is really a prison narrative. Trapped within Gilead's system and confined to the domestic spaces of the home (which frequently means her room), nevertheless Offred claims her freedom by her refusals. She refuses to forget her past or her own name, she refuses to believe in biological reductionism, and she refuses to give up hope of getting out of her present situation. She knows what she needs to pay attention to: 'What I need is perspective. The illusion of depth . . . Otherwise you live in the moment. Which is not where I want to be' (Chapter 24).

Offred's greatest psychological resource is her faculty of double vision, for she is a survivor from the past, and it is her power to remember which enables her to survive in the present. It is not only through flashbacks that she reconstructs the past (though these are her most effective escape routes from isolation, loneliness and boredom), but even when she walks down the road she sees everything through a double exposure, with the past superimposed upon the present, or to use her own layered image from Chapter 1, as a 'palimpsest' where the past gives depth to the present. She has perfected the technique of simultaneously inhabiting two spaces: her Handmaid's space (or lack of it) and the freer, happier spaces of memory.

Just as she refuses to forget her life before Gilead and her lost family who belong to that past, so she refuses to give up her own name. Though she is forbidden to use it, she keeps it like a buried treasure, as guarantee of her other identity ('I keep the knowledge of this name like something hidden, some treasure I'll come back to dig up, one day' – Chapter 14). She gives her real name as a love token to Nick, and he in turn uses it as an exchange of faith when he comes for her with the black van ('He calls me by my real name. Why should this mean anything?' – Chapter 46). Offred does not trust the reader with her real name, however, which is a sign of her wariness in a precarious situation, though there is a fascinating essay by a Canadian critic, Constance Rooke, which argues that it is coded into the text and that Offred's real name is June.

What is most attractive about Offred is her lively responsiveness to the world around her. She is sharply observant of physical details in her surroundings, she is curious and likes to explore, and she has a very lyrical response to the Commander's Wife's beautiful garden. She observes its seasonal changes closely, for that garden represents for her all the natural fecundity and beauty that are denied by the regime but which flourish unchecked outside the window. It is also a silent testimonial to her own resistance:

> There is something subversive about this garden of Serena's, a sense of buried things bursting upwards, wordlessly, into the light, as if to point, to say: Whatever is silenced will clamour to be heard, though silently. A Tennyson garden, heavy with scent . . .
> (Chapter 25)

Her response to the moonlight is equally imaginative, though noticeably tinged with irony, which is one of her most distinctive characteristics:

> a wishing moon, a sliver of ancient rock, a goddess, a wink. The moon is a stone and the sky is full of deadly hardware, but oh God, how beautiful anyway. (Chapter 17)

Offred consistently refuses to be bamboozled by the rhetoric of Gilead, for she believes in the principle of making distinctions between things and in the precise use of words, just as she continues to believe in the value of every individual. Of the men in her life she says:

> Each one remains unique, there is no way of joining them together. They cannot be exchanged, one for the other. They cannot replace each other. (Chapter 30)

It is this sharpness of mind which informs her wittily critical view of her present situation, as in the satisfaction she gets out of teasing the young guard at the gate. 'I enjoy the power; power of a dog bone, passive but there' (Chapter 4).

Her attitude is discreetly subversive but never openly rebellious. She watches for those moments of instability when human responses break through official surfaces. Offred is mischievous, but, more seriously, she yearns for communication and trust between people instead of mutual suspicion and isolation. Ironically enough, her fullest human relationship in Gilead is her 'arrangement' with the Commander. This provides her with a 'forbidden oasis', for it is in their Scrabble games that Offred is at her liveliest and her most conventionally feminine. In his study, Offred and the Commander relate to each other by old familiar social and sexual codes, which alleviates the loneliness both feel. It is after her first evening that Offred does something she has never done before in the novel: she laughs out loud, partly at the absurdity of it all, but partly out of a reawakening of her own high spirits. Yet she is too intelligent ever to forget that it is only a game or a replay of the past in parodic form, and her outing to Jezebel's confirms this. For all its glitter, her purple sequined costume, like the evening, is a shabby masquerade, and in the clear light of day she is left sitting with 'a handful of crumpled stars' in her lap (Chapter 46).

Living in a terrorist state, Offred is, of course, always anxious and afraid. She is always alert to the glint of danger, as in her first unexpected encounter with Nick in the dark where fear and sexual risk exert a powerful charge which runs through the novel to its end. Their love represents the forbidden combination of desire and rebellion, and it is through that relationship that Offred manages to find new hope for the future and even to accommodate herself to reduced circumstances in the present, like a pioneer who has given up the Old World and come to the wilderness of a new one: 'I said, I have made a life for myself, here, of a sort. That must have been what the settlers' wives thought' (Chapter 41). Offred shows through her detailed psychological narrative how she can survive traumas of loss and bereavement and how she manages to elude the constraints of absolute authority.

We know little about her physical appearance because the only time she ever mentions it is when she is at her most bizarre, in her red habit with her white winged cap or in her purple sequined costume at Jezebel's. But we know a great deal about her mind and feelings and her sense of wry humour. We also know that she is a highly self-conscious narrator and that she is aware of contradictions and failings within herself. She knows that she lacks Moira's flamboyant courage, and she accuses herself of cowardice and unreliability, just as at the end she feels guilty for having betrayed the household who imprisoned her. Yet, despite her own self-doubts, Offred manages to survive with dignity and to embrace the possibility of her escape with hope. Her narrative remains a witness to the freedom and resilience of the human spirit.

It is worth making the point that in this first-person narrative Offred is central and everyone else is seen through her eyes, presented in a discontinuous sequence of vivid scenic units or sketches. As readers we then attempt to assemble these fragments in order to reconstruct believable characters. Like Offred or Professor Pieixoto, we too are involved in an exercise of reconstruction.

Serena Joy, the Commander's Wife

Unlike all the other Wives, Serena Joy is more than just a member of a class in the hierarchy of Gileadean women, for she has a name of her own and a past history. She is also the most powerful female presence in Offred's daily life, so Offred has plenty of opportunity to observe her at close quarters.

As an elderly childless woman she has to agree to the grotesque system of polygamy practised in Gilead and to shelter a Handmaid in her home, but it is plain that she resents this arrangement keenly as a violation of her marriage, and a continual reminder of her own crippled condition and fading feminine charms. The irony of the situation is made clear when Offred remembers Serena Joy's past history, first as a child singing star on a gospel television show, and later as a media personality speaking up for ultra-conservative domestic policies and the sanctity of the home. Now, as Offred maliciously remarks, Serena is trapped in the very ideology on which she had based her popularity: 'She stays in her home, but it doesn't seem to agree with her' (Chapter 8).

Serena's present life is a parody of the Virtuous Woman: her only place of power is her own sitting-room, she is estranged from her husband, jealous of her Handmaid, and has nothing to do except knit scarves for soldiers and gossip with her cronies or listen to her young voice on the gramophone. The only space for Serena's self-expression is her garden, and even that she cannot tend without the help of her husband's chauffeur. If flowers are important to Offred, so are they too to Serena, and she often sits alone in her 'subversive garden', knitting or smoking.

To see the world from Serena's perspective is to shift the emphasis of Offred's narrative, for these two women might be seen not as opposites but as doubles. They both want a child, and the attention of them both focuses on the Commander of whom Serena is very possessive: 'As for my husband, she said, he's just that. My husband. I want that to be perfectly clear. Till death do us part. It's final.' (Chapter 3).

Offred seldom knows what Serena is thinking, though there are indications of her attitudes and tastes in the jewels and the perfume she wears and in the funishings of her house: 'hard lust for quality, soft sentimental cravings' as Offred uncharitably puts it (Chapter 14). There is also evidence of a certain toughness in Serena's cigarette-smoking and her use of slang, not to mention her suggestion that Offred, unknown to the Commander, should sleep with Nick in order to conceive the child she is supposed to produce: 'She's actually smiling, coquettishly even; there's a hint of her former small-screen mannequin's allure, flickering over her face like momentary static' (Chapter 31). But Serena has her revenges too: she has deliberately withheld from Offred the news of her lost daughter and her photograph which Offred has been longing for.

By a curious twist, Serena occupies the role of the wife in a very conventional plot about marital infidelity, as well as in the privileged Gileadean sense. She is one of the points in the triangular relationship which develops between Offred and the Commander: 'The fact is that I'm his mistress . . . Sometimes I think she knows' (Chapter 26). Actually, she does not know until she finds the purple costume and the lipstick on her cloak. It is a cliché-like situation, but Serena's own pain of loss goes beyond this conventional pattern: ' "Behind my back," she says. "You could have left me something." ' Offred wonders, 'Does she love him, after all?' (Chapter 45).

Serena is still there in her house, standing anxiously beside the Commander at the end as Offred is led out the door. Her farewell to Offred is wifely in an old-fashioned sense which has none of the pieties of Gilead: ' "Bitch," she says. "After all he did for you" ' (Chapter 46).

Other Commanders' Wives

The other Wives have no individuality. They exist as a gaggle of gossips in blue, for Offred knows nothing of their lives apart from overhearing snatches of their conversation at Birth Days, Prayvaganzas or social visits, when they make scandalous comments about their Handmaids. Only the Wife of Warren achieves a moment of grotesque individuality when she is seen sitting on the Birth Stool behind Janine, 'wearing white cotton socks, and bedroom slippers, blue ones made of fuzzy material, like toilet-seat covers' (Chapter 21). There is also one other unfortunate Wife who is hanged at the Salvaging, but Offred does not know what her crime was: Was it murder? Was it adultery? 'It could always be that. Or attempted escape' (Chapter 42).

Moira

Moira, Offred's best friend, always known by her own name because she never becomes a Handmaid, is strongly individual, although she is also a type of the female rebel. This is a position which can be viewed in two ways, and both of them are illustrated here. From Offred's point of view Moira is the embodiment of female heroism, swashbuckling and irreverent, though from the Gileadean authorities' point of view she is a 'loose woman', a criminal element, and her story follows the conventional fictional pattern of such rebellious figures: she ends up (as far as Offred knows) as a prostitute in Jezebel's. Even here, Moira manages to express her dissidence, for she remains a declared lesbian and her costume is a deliberate travesty of feminine sexual allure, as Offred notices when she meets her again on her night out with the Commander. Moira's own wryly comic comment on it is, 'I guess they thought it was me' (Chapter 38).

Like Offred, Moira is a denizen of the permissive society, a trendy student at Offred's college who wears purple overalls and leaves her unfinished paper on 'Date Rape' to go for a beer. She is totally committed to separatist feminism and much more astute about sexual politics than Offred. She is also an activist in the Gay Rights movement, working for a women's collective at the time of the Gilead coup. When she is brought into the Rachel and Leah Centre she cannot be terrorised into even outward conformity; instead she tries to escape and succeeds on her second attempt. She manages to escape disguised as an Aunt. Always funny and ironic, to the other women at the Centre she represents all that they would like to do but would not dare:

> Moira was our fantasy. We hugged her to us, she was with us in secret, a giggle; she was lava beneath the crust of daily life. In the light of Moira, the Aunts were less fearsome and more absurd.
> (Chapter 22)

Moira's tragedy is that her energy and courage cannot be accommodated within Gilead, yet the regime will not let her escape. After eight months at liberty, she is finally recaptured and sent to Jezebel's, which is another form of imprisonment where she expects to remain for three or four years before being shipped off to the Colonies. She tells Offred her story in the women's washroom at Jezebel's white smoking a borrowed cigarette, but she tells it as an adventure yarn without any mention of the punishments she suffered for her rebellion. She is a courageous presence; she never loses her aura of fantasy for Offred, who wishes she could tell of how 'she blew up Jezebel's, with fifty Commanders inside'. Moira's, however, is one of the unfinished stories embedded in this narrative: 'I don't know how she ended, or even if she did, because I never saw her again' (Chapter 38).

Offred's mother

Offred's mother's life belongs to the history of the feminist movement which is being recorded in this novel, for she joined the Women's Liberation Movement of the 1960s and 70s, campaigning for women's sexual and social freedom. As an older woman she continued to be a political activist, and at the time of the Gileadean take-over she disappeared. Only much later does Offred learn that she has been condemned as an Unwoman and sent to the Colonies.

Like Moira, and possessing the same kind of energy, Offred's mother resists classification. In an odd way she even resists being dead, for she makes two startling appearances in the present, both times on film at the Rachel and Leah Centre. On one occasion Offred is shocked to see her as a young woman marching toward her in a pro-abortion march, and later Moira reports seeing her as an old woman working as slave labour in the Colonies.

Offred's mother is, however, more than a feminist icon. She haunts her daughter's memory, and gradually Offred comes to understand her mother's independence of mind and to admire her courage. Her mother is evoked in a series of kaleidoscopic images: at a feminist pornographic book burning (Chapter 7), with a bruised face after an abortion riot (Chapter 28), and as an elderly woman proudly defending her position as a single parent to Offred's husband, while accusing her daughter of naivety and political irresponsibility. It is her jaunty language which Offred remembers as distinguishing her mother:

A man is just a woman's strategy for making other women. Not that your father wasn't a nice guy and all, but he wasn't up to fatherhood. Not that I expected it of him. Just do the job, then you can bugger off, I said, I make a decent salary, I can afford daycare. So he went to the coast and sent Christmas cards. He had beautiful blue eyes though.   (Chapter 20)

An embarrassing but heroic figure, this is the woman whom her daughter misses when it is all too late, though Offred continues her dialogue with her mother in her own mind as a way of keeping her mother alive:

Mother, I think. Wherever you may be. Can you hear me? You wanted a women's culture. Well, now there is one. It isn't what you meant, but it exists. Be thankful for small mercies.
                                                                        (Chapter 21)

Finally Offred tries to lay her mother to rest, but without success: 'I've mourned for her already. But I will do it again, and again' (Chapter 39).

Aunts: Aunt Elizabeth, Aunt Helena, Aunt Lydia, Aunt Sara

The Aunts, like the Wives, the Marthas, the Econowives and most of the Handmaids, are not presented as individual characters, but as members of a class or group, every group representing a different female role within Gilead. With their names derived from pre-Gileadean women's products, the Aunts are the older women who are the female collaborators acting on the orders of the patriarchy to train and police Handmaids in an endeavour to reinstate traditional gender roles. They are a paramilitary organisation, as is signified by their khaki uniforms and their cattle prods, and, as propagandists of the regime, they tell distorted tales of women's lives in the pre-Gileadean past. The villainesses of the novel, they are responsible for the most gruesome cruelties, like the female Salvagings and the Particicutions, as well as for individual punishments at the Rachel and Leah Centre.

Only Aunt Lydia is individuated, and that is by her peculiar viciousness masquerading under a genteel feminine exterior: 'Aunt Lydia thought she was very good at feeling for other people' (Chapter 8). When Offred hears her voice over the loudspeaker at the female Salvaging, she feels full of hate (Chapter 42). As a particularly sadistic tormentor, Aunt Lydia is an awful warning that a women's culture is no guarantee of sisterhood as Offred's mother's generation of feminists had optimistically assumed, but that it is also necessary to take account of some women's pathological inclinations towards violence and vindictiveness.

Handmaids: Ofglen and Ofwarren (Janine)

These two emerge as individuals from their stereotypical roles, one because of her courage and rebelliousness and the other because she is the conventional female victim figure. Both are casualties of the Gileadean system.

Ofglen has no past life that Offred knows about, but she does have a secret life as a member of the Mayday resistance movement which she confides to Offred after weeks as her shopping partner. There is nothing exceptional about her appearance except her mechanical quality which Offred notices when she turns around, 'as if she's voice-activated, as if she's on little oiled wheels' (Chapter 8). Offred is proved right in her suspicions, for under the disguise of Handmaid, Ofglen is a sturdy resistance fighter. She identifies the alleged rapist as 'one of ours' and knocks him out before the horrible Particicution begins. She also dies as a fighter, preferring to commit suicide when she sees the black van coming rather than betray her friends under torture. Offred learns this from her replacement, the 'new, treacherous Ofglen', who whispers the news to her on their shopping expedition.

Janine is a female victim in both her lives: before Gilead when she worked as a waitress and was raped by a gang of thugs, then as a Handmaid. At the Rachel and Leah Centre she is a craven figure on the edge of nervous collapse, and consequently one of Aunt Lydia's pets. Though she has her moment of triumph as the 'vastly pregnant' Handmaid Ofwarren in Chapter 5, she is also a victim of the system with which she has tried so hard to curry favour. Even at the Birth Day she is neglected as soon as the baby is born and left 'crying helplessly, burnt-out miserable tears' when her baby is taken away and given to the Wife (Chapter 21). There is no reward for Janine. Her baby is declared an Unbaby and destroyed because it is deformed; Janine becomes a pale shadow overwhelmed with guilt; finally, after the Particicution, when Offred sees her again, she has slipped over into madness.

Marthas: Cora and Rita

These female domestic servants are rather like Shakespeare's artisans, following their traditional pursuits and apparently unaffected by the social upheavals around them. Offred would like to gossip with the two Marthas in her household, Cora and Rita, but they are too afraid of losing their places to give her companionship. She thinks of their lives as ordinary and safe by contrast with her own, and she knows that to them she is just another 'household chore, one among many' (Chapter 8). Cora is the kinder of the two, for she actually believes in the value of a Handmaid's mission and hopes for a baby in their household, while Rita's attitude is a sterner one of old-fashioned moral disapproval.

It is Cora who brings Offred's breakfast and supper trays up to her room, and by the frequency of her appearances and her brief snatches of dialogue she is sketched in as a personality. She has her one moment of drama, when she finds Offred asleep in the cupboard and drops her tray, thinking that Offred has committed suicide like her predecessor whom Cora also found. She has her one moment of hope, when she thinks that Offred may be pregnant: 'It won't be long now, says Cora, doling out my monthly stack of sanitary napkins. Not long now, smiling at me shyly but also knowingly' (Chapter 41). At the end it is she whom Offred feels that she has betrayed: 'Cora has begun to cry. I was her hope, I've failed her. Now she will always be childless' (Chapter 46).

Econowives

The Econowives, those worn-looking women in striped dresses whose condition no social revolution seems to improve, make only three brief appearances. They are seen by Offred as a group at the Prayvaganza and the Salvaging, and she sees them once at a baby's funeral where they form a forlorn little procession coming down the street. One of these women at least expresses her feelings directly, for when she sees the two Handmaids, she turns aside and spits on the pavement (Chapter 8).

The Commander

The Commander is the most powerful authority figure in Offred's world. He is a high-ranking government official, at the top of the bureaucratic structure of Gilead according to Ofglen, and he is head of the household to which Offred is assigned. It is his first name which she takes, though whether as a slave or as a parody of the marriage service is never made clear. Yet he is an ambiguous figure, substantial but shadowy, whose motivations, like his career in Gilead, remain unclear to Offred; even in the 'Historical Notes' his identity remains uncertain.

As a Commander he wears a black uniform and is driven in a prestige car, a Whirlwind. He is an elderly man with 'straight neatly brushed silver hair' and a moustache and blue eyes. He is slightly stooped and his manner is mild (Chapter 15). As Offred observes him with his gold-rimmed glasses on his nose reading from the Bible before the monthly Ceremony, she thinks he looks 'like a midwestern bank president', an astute judgment, as he tells her much later that before Gilead he was in market research (Chapter 29). The image he presents is that of male power, isolated and benignly indifferent to domestic matters, which include his Wife and his Handmaid. This is, however, not entirely true, for Offred has seen him earlier on the day of the Ceremony, a figure lurking in the shadows outside her room, who tried to peer at her as she passed: 'Something has been shown to me, but what is it?' (Chapter 8).

It is only after the official Ceremony, performed by the Commander in full dress uniform and with his eyes shut, that Offred has the chance to get to know him a little and his stereotypical male power image begins to break down. It is he who asks her to visit him 'after hours' in his study, for he is a lonely man who desires friendship and intimacy with his Handmaid and not the serviceable monthly sex for which she has been allocated to him. In his Bluebeard's chamber, what he has to offer is not 'kinky sex' but Scrabble games and an appearance of 'normal life', with conversation and books and magazines, all of which he knows are forbidden to Handmaids. On his own private territory the Commander is an old-fashioned gentleman with an attractive sheepish smile, who treats Offred in a genially patronising way and gradually becomes quite fond of her. 'In fact he is positively daddyish' (Chapter 29). He seems to have the ability to compartmentalise his life (in a way that Offred cannot manage) so that he can separate her official role as sexual slave from her unofficial role as his companion. In many ways the Commander's motives and needs remain obscure to Offred, though they do manage to develop an amiable relationship, which from one point of view is bizarre and from another is entirely banal: 'The fact is that I'm his mistress' (Chapter 26).

Yet their relationship is still a game of sexual power politics in which the Commander holds most of the cards, as Offred never allows herself to forget. For all his gallantry, he remains totally trapped in traditional patriarchal assumptions, believing that these are 'Nature's norm' (Chapter 34) and allow exploitation of women, as his comments and conduct at Jezebel's suggest. When he takes her upstairs there, she resists him:

> Alone at last, I think. The fact is that I don't want to be alone with him, not on a bed. I'd rather have Serena there too. I'd rather play Scrabble. (Chapter 39)

Their private sexual encounter ends in 'futility and bathos' and is strongly contrasted with Offred's meeting with Nick later that same evening.

As she leaves his house for the last time, Offred sees the Commander standing at the sitting-room door, looking old, worried and helpless. Possibly he is expecting his own downfall, for nobody is invulnerable in Gilead. Offred has her revenge, for the balance of power between them has shifted: 'Possibly he will be a security risk, now. I am above him, looking down; he is shrinking' (Chapter 46).

The academics go to some trouble later to establish the Commander's identity: he may have been 'Frederick R. Waterford' or 'B. Frederick Judd'. Waterford, it is revealed, had a background in market research (which seems most likely), while the more sinister Judd was a military strategist who worked for the CIA. Both of them 'met their ends, probably soon after the events our author describes'.

Nick

Nick is presented as the central figure of Offred's romantic fantasy, for he is the mysterious dark stranger who is her rescuer through love. He also has a place in her real world, of course, as the Commander's chauffeur and the Commander's Wife's gardener. He 'has a French face, lean, whimsical, all planes and angles, with creases around the mouth where he smiles' (Chapter 4) and a general air of irreverence, wearing his cap at a jaunty angle, whistling while he polishes the car, and winking at Offred the first day he sees her. At the household prayers he presses his foot against hers, and she feels a surge of sensual warmth which she dare not acknowledge. In the daytime he is rather a comic figure but at night he is transformed into Offred's romantic lover, the embodiment of sexual desire. This transformation is made all the more piquant because he is always acting under orders, either as the Commander's messenger or as the lover chosen for Offred by the Commander's Wife.

From their first unexpected encounter in the dark sitting-room (Chapter 17) theirs is a silent exchange which carries an unmistakable erotic charge. It is Nick's hands which make his declaration

> His fingers move, feeling my arm under the night-gown sleeve, as if his hand won't listen to reason. It's so good, to be touched by someone, to be felt so greedily, to feel so greedy.
>
> (Chapter 17)

At night he stares longingly up at Offred's window and she stares back: 'I have no rose to toss, he has no lute. But it's the same kind of hunger' (Chapter 30).

As a subordinate, Nick, like Offred, has to remain passive until ordered by the Commander's Wife to go to bed with Offred. On that occasion his attitude is not directly described but veiled by

Offred's three different versions of that meeting. Certainly she falls in love with him, and in defiance of danger she returns many times to his room across the dark lawn on her own. Towards the end, she tells him that she is pregnant. Nevertheless her description of their love-making is suggestive rather than explicitly erotic, and Nick tends to remain a shadowy, mysterious figure. Even at the end when he appears with the Eyes to take her away, Offred really knows so little about him that she almost accuses him of having betrayed her, until he calls her by her real name and begs her to trust him. Ever elusive, he is the only member of the household not there to see her depart. We want to believe that Nick was in love with Offred, and we must assume from the 'Historical Notes' that he did rescue her and that he was a member of Mayday resistance. However, as a character he is very lightly sketched and it is his function as romantic lover which is most significant.

Luke

Luke is one of the Missing Persons in this novel. Probably dead before the narrative begins, he haunts Offred's memory until he fades like a ghost as her love affair with Nick develops. He is the one person Offred leaves out when she tells the story of her past life to Nick (Chapter 41), though she is still worrying about him at the end (Chapter 44).

He is also the most fragmented character in the text, appearing briefly as a name in Chapter 2, and then gradually taking on an identity as Offred's lover, husband and the father of her child. He is a figure whose life story stopped for Offred at a traumatic point in the past: 'Stopped dead in time, in mid-air, among the trees back there, in the act of falling' (Chapter 35). Through her reconstruction Luke appears as a late twentieth-century 'liberated man', full of courage and humour and remembered by Offred entirely in his domestic relations with her. He is an older man who has been married before, so that there is an ironic parallel drawn between him and the Commander. Offred remembers their affair when she goes with the Commander to Jezebel's, for it is the hotel where she and Luke used to go (Chapter 37). She retains the memory of a strong loving partner, and her detailed recollections are of Luke cooking and joking with her mother, of lying in bed with her before their daughter was born, of collecting their daughter from school. We never know what Luke's job was, but Offred recalls his supportive behaviour when she lost her job at the time of the Gileadean take-over and her resentment against him for being a man (Chapter 28).

Luke figures insistently in Offred's recurring nightmare of their failed escape attempt, not only in that final image of him lying shot face down in the snow, but also in her recollections of his careful preparations and his coolly courageous attempt to take his family to freedom over the Canadian border. His afterlife in the novel is very much the result of Offred's anxieties about what might have happened to him: Is he dead, or in prison? Did he escape? Will he send her a message and help her to escape back into their old family life? 'It's this message, which may never arrive, that keeps me alive. I believe in the message' (Chapter 18). It is also her hope of this message which keeps the image of Luke alive. The anxieties we may feel for his fate are projections of Offred's own.

The doctor

He appears once, in Chapter 11; or rather he partially appears, for Offred sees only his hand and the upper part of his face above his gauze mask during her monthly medical check-up. He is one of the male voices of authority in Gilead, where as spokesman for the biological definition of femaleness he is bound to be important. Offred notices him because he transgresses his medical role by his whispered and totally illegal offer to make her pregnant. It is not clear whether he does it out of kindness or as part of a male power game based on the exploitation of women. When Offred refuses him she does so warily in order not to offend him, for she knows that his report could make all the difference between life and death for her. He is an ambiguous figure, another representative of the patriarchal structure of Gilead.

Professor Pieixoto

Professor James Darcy Pieixoto of the University of Cambridge, England (not Cambridge, Massachusetts, where *The Handmaid's Tale* is set), is not a character as such but a male narrative voice which attempts to impose an 'objective' historical interpretation on Offred's story at a Canadian academic conference on Gilead held in the year 2195. As one of the two archivists responsible for the transcription, editing and publication of Offred's tale, he is the representative of authoritative scholarship. His objectivity, however, is seriously undermined by the sexist jokes he makes and his evident sympathy for the male social architects of Gilead. Though his scholarly procedures are not in question, his line of inquiry is biased against ever finding out anything about Offred, for his interests are the traditional ones of male power politics: who was Offred's Commander? How can Gileadean policy be related to historical precedents? The predictable result is that he fails to understand Offred's story and then blames her – and history – for his own blindness. By contrast with her tale of suffering and survival, the Professor's voice sounds very Olympian and indifferent. His main function is possibly to irritate readers into forming their own interpretations of Offred's little narrative in contrast to his grand historical narrative.

References and allusions

The allusions to Western cultural history in *The Handmaid's Tale* are extremely wide-ranging, stretching from the Bible to late twentieth-century feminism and environmental issues. There are also references to seventeenth-century American Puritanism, the slave trade, Nazism and pornographic films, as well as motifs from fairy tales, quotations from Shakespeare, John Milton, René Descartes, Alfred Lord Tennyson, Sigmund Freud and Karl Marx. The 'Historical Notes' add another layer of reference in an effort to set Gilead within an international history of totalitarianism and various forms of institutional oppression. This formidable range of references is part of Margaret Atwood's strategy for constructing her modern anti-utopia, and it is also a mark of her own high level of cultural literacy. But the novel is not at all daunting, for it uses allusions very wittily, one of its functions being to mesh together social details with which we are all familiar in order to show us how they might be shaped into a pattern for a future which we would choose to avoid.

Many of these allusions are annotated in the Notes in Section 2. Here attention will be concentrated on the biblical references and their significance. Gilead's social principles are based on the Old Testament, where patriarchal authority is justified as the law of God. There are far more references to the Old than to the New Testament, a common feature of more extreme sects where the archaic language of patriarchy is used as a mechanism for social control. The patriarch Jacob is the state hero, and the name Gilead is closely associated with Jacob, for that was the place where he set up his heap of stones as witness to God and where he established his household, his lineage and his flocks and herds. (See the note on Gilead in the detailed summary of Chapter 5, Part 2, p. 16 above).

The first quotation of the three in the epigraph directs our attention to Genesis 30:1–3, which is the beginning of the story about Jacob and his two wives Rachel and Leah and their two handmaids who are required to produce children for them. As the basis of the novel it is reiterated many times in the text, most notably in the family Bible reading before the monthly Ceremony, and there are echoes of it in the name of the Rachel and Leah Centre and in Offred's remark that 'Give me children, or else I die' can have more than one meaning for her as a Handmaid (Chapter 11). As already mentioned, the New Testament is less in evidence, though there is one long passage quoted (1 Timothy 2:9–15) which is used at the mass marriage ceremony in Chapter 34 as part of Gilead's propaganda about male domination and female submission.

In such a society biblical references pervade every level of discourse. Gilead's leaders understand very well the importance of language as the main instrument of ideological control, and indeed it is just as repressive an instrument as the army and the police, and a great deal more insidious because rituals of naming determine the way we think about our lives. The law enforcers themselves are named after Old Testament figures, whether they are 'Guardian Angels' or the 'Eyes of the Lord'.

On the domestic level women's roles are given biblical significance, as in the case of the Handmaids, of course, but also in that of the female servants who become 'Marthas' after the woman who served Christ. (There is an amusing break in the rhetoric with the references to the 'Econowives', whose naming seems more influenced by late twentieth-century advertising than by Scripture.) With 'Jezebel's' as the name of the state-run brothel, however, Gilead's misogyny is made plain, for Jezebel's name occurs in both Old and New Testaments, always as whore or sorceress. This name suggests the scandal of female sexuality which Gilead can neither condone nor do without.

In a country where God is treated as a 'national resource', biblical names filter into the commercial world. The car brand names available are 'Behemoth', 'Whirlwind' or 'Chariot' (instead of 'Mustang' or 'Avenger', for example?) and shops have been renamed with pictorial signs which pick up biblical texts like 'Lilies of the Field' (a dress shop) and 'All Flesh' (a butcher's shop). It is an ironic comment on the fact that such naming is only the most superficial sanctification of shopping by coupons, for everything is rationed in Gilead.

Perhaps the funniest misappropriation is Aunt Lydia's exhortation to the Handmaids, which she claims is from St Paul: 'From each according to her ability, to each according to his needs' (Chapter 20). These words are not in the Bible at all; they are a garbled version of Karl Marx's description of systems of production, though they do make the point that Aunt Lydia wished to stress about service roles. In a similar way the Freudian reference to 'Pen Is Envy' (Chapter 29) and the Miltonic reference (Chapter 4) also emphasise women's inferiority and subservience to men.

The conclusion to be drawn is that Gilead uses biblical references to underwrite patriarchal interests, but it uses them very selectively and sometimes inaccurately. The Word is in the mouths of men only, just as the Bible is kept locked up and only Commanders are allowed to read it. Even the hymns are edited, and Moira's dissenting version of 'There is a Balm in Gilead' (Chapter 34) is muffled in the massed choir of the Handmaids. Offred prays quite often in her own private way, saying her version of the Lord's Prayer (Chapter 30) or crying out to God in despair (Chapter 45), but again her voice is muted. Gilead's official discourse is a hybridised rhetoric which combines biblical language with traces of American capitalist phrases ('In God We Trust' is the motto on the dollar bill), Marxism and feminism. It uses and abuses the Bible in the same way as it uses the slogans of the liberal ideology it has overthrown, that is, selectively and inconsistently.

Language and imagery

The language of *The Handmaid's Tale* is apparently simple and economical. There are very few words that need to be checked in a dictionary (apart from those words in the Scrabble game) and sentences tend to follow conventional syntactic structures. But it is worth remembering that Atwood is a poet as well as a novelist and that she brings the poetic resources of imagery and fantasy to her fiction, as well as the ability to write in a variety of styles. This novel is actually a stylistic *tour de force*, though so subtly constructed that on a first reading we might well think it simple.

Several different kinds of language are used. First, there is Offred's own language which she uses to tell her private experiences, with echoes of her remembered dialogues with Moira, her mother and Luke and her conversations with the Commander. Indeed the forthright, slangy nature of the speech of Moira and Offred's mother, the two leading feminists in the book, might be classed as a sub-language within Offred's own, which she remembers with delight. By contrast there is Gilead's official language (consistently rejected and exposed by Offred for the fraud it perpetrates) which is used by the Aunts at the Rachel and Leah Centre, at official ceremonies like the Prayvaganza, and imposed on the Handmaids in their ritual exchanges as well as on the populace at large in the renamings and slogans devised by the regime. This language, with its texture of biblical allusion and deceit, is likely to cause most problems for contemporary readers. There is a third, completely different language used by Professor Pieixoto in the 'Historical Notes' through which the novelist satirises the kind of pretentious discourse which might be used in a paper at an academic conference. (Sadly, she is suggesting that these things might not be very different even in two hundred years time!)

It is Offred's voice transcribed into text which situates her as an individual woman grounded in place and time, whose identity transcends that of her Handmaid's role. Through the language she uses, rather than the events of the story she tells, Offred convinces us of her resistance to Gilead's values. Offred's outer life is very constricted and drained of emotion, but her inner life has an energy and lyricism which enable her to survive emotionally as well as physically in the stony soil of Gilead. There is, as we might expect, a marked difference between the language she uses to record her muted everyday life, and the language of her real life of feeling and memory, which is expressed through a richly worked vocabulary of images. These register her entirely different perception of herself and her world from the one imposed by Gilead. You will notice that there are a small number of recurrent images which form patterns or 'image clusters' throughout her narrative. They derive from the human body (hands, feet, faces, eyes, blood, wombs), also from non-human nature (flowers, gardens, changing seasons, colour and light – especially moonlight). Offred's images, all related to nature and organic processes, constitute a 'feminine' language that works in opposition to Gilead's polluted technological nightmare and its accompanying rhetoric.

To see how Offred's language works, four passages will be discussed, each one quite different, though all containing the same key motifs. The first passage, the opening paragraph of Chapter 2, is Offred's description of her room in the Commander's house, which conveys to us an immediate impression of enclosed space and a pared-down existence:

A chair, a table, a lamp. Above, on the white ceiling, a relief ornament in the shape of a wreath, and in the centre of it a blank space, plastered over, like the place in a face where the eye has been taken out. There must have been a chandelier, once. They've removed anything you could tie a rope to.

A window, two white curtains. Under the window, a window seat with a little cushion. When the window is partly open – it only opens partly – the air can come in and make the curtains move. I can sit in the chair, or on the window seat, hands folded, and watch this. Sunlight comes in through the window too, and falls on the floor, which is made of wood, in narrow strips, highly polished. I can smell the polish. There's a rug on the floor, oval, of braided rags. This is the kind of touch they like: folk art, archaic, made by women, in their spare time, from things that have no further use. A return to traditional values. Waste not want not. I am not being wasted. Why do I want?

This passage begins as an impersonal inventory of solid objects set side by side. Then the narrator lifts her eyes to the ceiling, only to confront blankness in the middle of a plaster wreath, signifying absence and death. Surely there was a light-fitting here, and why has it been removed? As the description continues, the sense of constriction gets stronger, for this is a room in which nothing happens. Yet the breeze does manage to come in and so too does the sunlight. Then the narrator's eyes move to the polished floor and focus on the handmade rug which might be seen as emblematic evidence of old-fashioned values of thrift and domestic work. As Offred thinks of the proverb 'Waste not, want not' which seems to confirm these values, she suddenly starts to question them as she plays with the words 'waste' and 'want', recalling their different meanings when applied not to old rags but to a human being.

Spoken by a woman in isolation who is powerless against 'them', the rule makers, this is a prose that appears to be stripped of emotion until the last question. Yet that is not quite the case, as the simile of the blinded eye and the reference to the hanging rope indicate. Pain and the threat of death are encoded here, as well as a longing for more than what this minimal existence provides. This scenario is emblematic of a Handmaid's life, with its 'amputated speech' and restricted movement, where a woman is confined to traditional interior domestic spaces. As we might expect, the cluster of images centring on the plaster ceiling wreath, the white curtains and the room are developed through the story, for this is the space where Offred's present life is grounded. It is also the place from which she devises an escape route every night back into the wider spaces of memory. A significant part of Offred's strategy of resistance is to acknowledge her constricted life as she draws on the limited materials available to her, which she then transforms through the exercise of imagination and memory.

As Offred says when commenting on her story, 'I've tried to put some of the good things in as well. Flowers, for instance' (Chapter 41). She is particularly attracted to the Commander's Wife's garden, which, though it is enclosed by a brick wall and not available to her to sit in, represents a different space outside. She is fascinated by the garden as an image of the natural world which celebrates the beauty and fertility already lost in the public world of Gilead. When she talks about the garden she always says 'we' and 'our', signalling her private sense of possessing its beauty. This is the one spot in the

household where she feels a strong sense of belonging. In the following passage, Offred's rhapsody over the garden in its summer glory
gives her a moment of release when she transcends her physical
constraints and enters into the otherness of the natural world:

> The willow is in full plumage and is no help, with its insinuating
> whispers. *Rendezvous*, it says, *terraces*; the sibilants run up my
> spine, a shiver as if in fever. The summer dress rustles against the
> flesh of my thighs, the grass grows underfoot, at the edges of my
> eyes there are movements, in the branches; feathers, flittings,
> grace notes, tree into bird, metamorphosis run wild. Goddesses
> are possible now and the air suffuses with desire. Even the bricks
> of the house are softening, becoming tactile; if I leaned against
> them they'd be warm and yielding. It's amazing what denial can
> do. Did the sight of my ankle make him lightheaded, faint, at the
> check-point yesterday, when I dropped my pass and let him pick
> it up for me? No handkerchief, no fan, I use what's handy.
>
> (Chapter 25)

Offred experiences the garden as a place of living colour and
movement, a place of delightful temptation, where she hears the
willow tree whispering its traditional promises of romantic trysts. In
this world of heightened physical sensation she becomes aware of
her own body inside her red dress, with the same sensitivity as she
feels the grass growing and hears the birds singing. The dynamic
natural rhythms are so powerful that she imagines that she is actually
observing the process of 'metamorphosis' in which things change
from one shape into another, so that the rustling leaves and fluttering
birds merge together and the tree becomes the bird 'in full plumage'.
In her mind this process is associated with Ovid's *Metamorphoses*,
the early first-century Latin poem about supernatural transformations of human beings into trees or animals. The word 'goddesses'
focuses images of myth and desire, and as Offred watches, everything
comes alive, even the brick walls which become soft and warm like
flesh. Of course Offred suspects that her rhapsody is at least in part
a sublimation of her own frustrated desires, and she remembers the
way in which she teased the young guard who was on duty the day
before, wryly admitting the limited props available for her short
flirtatious scenario.

This garden appears to Offred as a feminised emblem of sexual
desire. Her imagination is not attached to the Christian image of the
enclosed paradise presided over by the Virgin Mary as the image of
female virtue, even though Serena Joy, whose garden it is, wears a
blue gardening dress, the Virgin's colour. Instead for Offred it is a
pagan garden presided over by goddesses, and being in the garden

evokes a heady combination of feelings filtered through a literary imagination which enacts its own magical transformations. It is a kind of nature mysticism where Offred herself undergoes a 'metamorphosis', changing from Handmaid to ripening fruit like a 'melon on a stem' attached to a natural life-giving source, as she becomes for a moment a part of this pulsating organic world.

Throughout her narrative Offred pays close attention to her body and its sensations, as Gilead demands its Handmaids should. The difference is that, despite Gilead, she continues to regard her body as her own private territory and writes about it in terms significantly different from patriarchal prescriptions. There is a remarkable passage where she lies in the bath on the evening of the monthly Ceremony, and through an intense meditation on what she calls 'the droolings of the flesh' achieves another moment of transcendence of human limits, not unlike the one in the garden. This time she transforms the dark spaces inside her body into cosmic space by a powerful use of metaphor:

> Now the flesh arranges itself differently. I'm a cloud, congealed around a central object, the shape of a pear, which is hard and more real than I am and glows red within its translucent wrapping. Inside it is a space, huge as the sky at night and dark and curved like that, though black-red rather than black. Pinpoints of light swell, sparkle, burst and shrivel within it, countless as stars. Every month there is a moon, gigantic, round, heavy, an omen. It transits, pauses, continues on and passes out of sight, and I see despair coming towards me like famine. To feel that empty, again, again. I listen to my heart, wave upon wave, salty and red, continuing on and on, marking time. (Chapter 13)

Offred begins by thinking about her changing sense of her own body, for she no longer thinks of it as the agent of her own will. It has become a cloud of flesh massed round the inner space of her womb, which is now her most significant physical feature. To describe the rhythms of her menstrual cycle she uses the image of the night sky studded with stars and traversed by the moon waxing and waning. Accurate in every detail as analogy, this is also a transforming metaphor, as the dark womb space expands until it assumes cosmic proportions. When the moon disappears, leaving the sky empty, Offred, not having conceived, is also left empty and drained of hope. The only issue will be blood, whose rhythm she feels beating through her like the sea, for this is her own dark female space where time is kept by the body: 'I tell time by the moon. Lunar, not solar' (Chapter 31). Through metaphor Offred resists Gilead's appropriation of her body. She also offers an alternative landscape to the night sky of Gilead streaked with searchlights.

Bodies, however, are made of flesh and can be wounded and broken, as happens so often in Gilead. It is this suffering and pain that Offred acknowledges through the imagery she uses to describe her story-telling process in the excerpt that follows, suggesting the conditions out of which her narrative is told:

> I'm sorry there is so much pain in this story. I'm sorry it's in fragments, like a body caught in crossfire or pulled apart by force. But there is nothing I can do to change it . . .
>
> Nevertheless it hurts me to tell it over, over again. Once was enough: wasn't once enough for me at the time? But I keep on going with this sad and hungry and sordid, this limping and muti-lated story, because after all I want you to hear it, as I will hear yours too if I ever get the chance, if I meet you or if you escape, in the future or in Heaven or in prison or underground, some other place. What they have in common is that they're not here. By telling you anything at all I'm at least believing in you, I believe you're there, I believe you into being. Because I'm telling you this story I will your existence. I tell, therefore you are.
>
> (Chapter 41)

If the preceding passage was 'writing the body', this last one might be described as writing the story as if it were a body. Offred begins by likening the structure of her story to a dismembered body, but then, shifting the focus to her subject matter, she presents her story personified as a victim of torture or as one of the walking wounded after a battle. Her story is an eye-witness to disaster, but it is also, as she recognises, a substitute for dialogue and an escape fantasy. As stories presuppose both tellers and listeners, so Offred's story-telling process invents her listeners in whom she needs to believe because she needs to believe in a world outside Gilead to which she hopes she will be able to escape one day. Her awareness of her strategy is plain in her deliberate address to readers as 'you' outside the text and outside Gilead. This is emphasised by her punning variant on Descartes's famous sentence: 'I think, therefore I am.' Offred resists the self-enclosure of this definition of humanness, just as she rejects Descartes's insistence on the absolute separation between thought and body. She shifts the emphasis to language and communication, setting up an interaction between 'I' and 'you'. Her prison narrative is presented as the only way of bridging the gap between an isolated self and the world outside. Story-telling becomes her means of personal survival, just as we find at the end that her story is her only means of survival within history. Her words remain long after her body has disappeared.

Offred's is indeed a narrative of resistance, challenging not only Gilead's perspective but also the misrepresentations of her experience in the future, for it illustrates the difference between a woman's private narrative of memory and the grand impersonal narrative of history. Having heard Offred's voice (resurrected by Professor Pieixoto's expertise with obsolete cassette tapes) we are unlikely to accept his scholarly gloss which consigns her, like Eurydice, to the world of the dead, or at best to the world of myth. We may not know her future but we do understand her present situation much better than the professor is willing to admit: Her story shows up the limits of Gilead's power just as it defies patriarchal appropriation two hundred years later, challenging us as readers to connect her 'then' with our 'now' in the hope of averting a nightmare like Gilead for our future.

Part 4

Hints for study

THIS NOVEL is a first-person narrative, like a diary or a letter, which tells the story from one woman's point of view. Because she is telling events in the present as they happen and because she has a very limited view of what is going on in Gilead, there is little sense of a forward-moving plot. Instead, we are very close to this woman's own thoughts and feelings, so that our main interest is likely to be a psychological one rather than an interest in narrative suspense. As you read it, you might try to think how different your response to the story would have been if it had been told by a third-person omniscient narrator (that is, by someone who knew the whole story and its outcome before beginning to tell it).

One of the first things we notice is the way the story shifts abruptly from one scene to another and from present time to the past, so that the narrator's present situation and her past history are only gradually revealed. Reading is an exercise of reconstruction as we piece together present details with fragments of remembered experience, revealed by flashbacks. At the beginning there are few flashbacks, for we, like the narrator, are trapped in present time. The first flashback occurs in Chapter 3 and there are brief references to Luke in Chapters 2 and 5. However it is in the 'Night' sections that the flashback technique is most obvious and most sustained, for this is Offred's 'time out' when she is free to wander back into her remembered past. It is here that we gain a sense of Offred as a powerful personal presence with a history. These are also the sections where Offred comments on the process of her story-telling as well as on her need to tell and reveals herself as a very self-conscious narrator, writing about writing. It is this self-reflexivity which is one of the distinctively contemporary features of this novel, and Offred comments quite frequently on the way in which story-telling takes personal experience and shapes it into narrative, so changing the raw materials of her life into fiction. It is a good idea when reading the novel to make a brief summary of every chapter, for this will enable you to see how inner psychological details and particulars of the external world are recorded. You will also be able to use this evidence to trace the mosaic method used in structuring the novel out of scenic units. Try to work out the advantages of organising chapters into the fifteen larger named sections of Offred's narrative.

In the nightmarish world of Gilead, there are so many references to social issues which we recognise from our own world that we find ourselves moving constantly between the 'now' of the novel and the 'now' of our own lives. Make a note of contemporary issues which strike you. (These will include issues relating to feminism and the anti-feminist backlash, surrogate mothers, abortion, pornography and social violence, issues concerning ecology and pollution, issues of nationalism, extreme right wing political movements and religious fanaticism.) What Margaret Atwood has done in her anti-utopia is to project a scenario warning us about what could happen if some of the current trends in our society were pushed to extremes. It is an interesting point about the topicality of utopias and anti-utopias that they are always responses to conditions that are causing anxiety at the time of writing, so that *The Handmaid's Tale* is not about apocalyptic threats of 'The Bomb' but about threats of ecological disaster. Many of us would survive this new kind of apocalypse but social organisations would most likely be radically different. *The Handmaid's Tale* is Atwood's version of what such a society might look like, just as it is also her strong warning against letting such things happen.

In many ways the ideas in this novel are more important than the characters – with the exception of Offred, who feels isolated and afraid most of the time. The other characters tend to function as members of groups or as representatives of certain ideological positions imposed by Gilead. However, as Offred insists, every individual is significant, whatever Gilead decrees, and her narrative does weave in particularities: she continually writes in other voices in sections of dialogue, in embedded stories and in remembered episodes. As a way of getting to know the other characters it is a good idea to put together the fragments of information about them scattered through Offred's narrative, as has been suggested in the section on 'Characters' in Part 3. Could you add more pieces of information to give a fuller characterisation of Moira or of the Commander, for example? Would you come to a different evaluation of Serena Joy from the one offered by Offred?

It is worth looking closely at the language of the novel in order to see the ways in which Offred manages to relieve the bleakness of her narrative. Consider her use of images relating to flowers and gardens or to the human body, all of which suggest a different way of relating to the world than the repressive official discourse of Gilead. This brings us to the use and the purpose of biblical allusions in the text. It is worth looking up these references in the Bible in order to see how selective they are, and how they offer a very partial reading of the Book of Genesis. This Book includes the stories of the Creation and of Adam and Eve as well as the story of Jacob and his wives and handmaids, but Gilead chooses only the latter and within it only those passages which support its oppressive patriarchal principles. Indeed you will notice that its rhetoric is actually very repetitive. Like any propaganda when it is examined closely, it represents a distortion of its sources in the interests of an official policy or ideological position. It might be seen as an abuse of the Bible rather than an endorsement of its teachings.

The 'Historical Notes' are not part of the Handmaid's tale, but they are part of the novel, so we need to consider how the abrupt shift to a different narrative voice and a different time perspective contributes to our understanding of Offred's story and of Atwood's project. (Make a list of the points that Professor Pieixoto makes in his academic paper, and also note the topics in Offred's narrative which he leaves out.) Why include these Notes, when they do not tell us what happened to Offred? Instead, they give us a general historical context for evaluating Gilead as a social experiment, and the professor as academic historian pushes Offred back into the past exactly as she feared official historians would do: 'From the point of view of future history, this kind, we'll be invisible' (Chapter 35). As we have been so closely involved with Offred we are likely to resent losing her in this broad survey, and we may feel that Professor Pieixoto neglects the most valuable elements of Offred's narrative which are its human particulars. Surely our irritation at this point is part of Atwood's intention? Of course she is saying that we should learn from the lessons of history, but she is also urging us to listen to the stories of people who are suffering and oppressed at this very moment, and not to pretend (like the professor) that they can be pushed comfortably out of the way. We end with a double perspective on the narrative, for it has been presented from both Offred's and Professor Pieixoto's points of view. Which do you prefer, and why?

Specimen questions

Here are a number of possible questions on the text, treating aspects of characterisation, themes, narrative technique, style and language, genre, and the story-teller's relation to society. Specimen answers are provided for three of them.

(1) In interpreting this novel, what matters more: a focus on character, or a focus on politics?
(2) '*The Handmaid's Tale* is a story about power.' Discuss.
(3) Compare and contrast Offred and Moira as feminist heroines in *The Handmaid's Tale*.

(4) In what ways can Offred's tale be described as a resistance narrative when Offred herself is neither a member of the Mayday resistance movement nor an obvious social dissident?

(5) 'Love? said the Commander . . . Falling in love, I said.' How significant are male–female relationships in *The Handmaid's Tale*?

(6) Discuss the role of the Aunts in *The Handmaid's Tale*.

(7) 'Doubled, I walk the street.' How is the concept of doubling or twinning used by Offred in her narrative?

(8) Offred may be the heroine of her own story, but there are many other heroines in her narrative. Discuss three of them and their function in *The Handmaid's Tale*.

(9) What are the effects of the first-person narrative on the reader of *The Handmaid's Tale*?

(10) Offred describes her narrative as 'this limping and mutilated story'. How does this image relate to *either* the content *or* the structure of *The Handmaid's Tale*?

(11) How are the 'Night' sections different from the rest of the novel, and what is their importance?

(12) Many of the principles of Gilead are based on Old Testament beliefs. Discuss Margaret Atwood's use of biblical allusions and their political significance in the novel.

(13) 'I've tried to put some of the good things in as well. Flowers, for instance, because where would we be without them?' Discuss Offred's vocabulary of images in the light of this statement.

(14) How does Margaret Atwood create an illusion of realism in her futuristic world of Gilead?

(15) What is the function of the 'Historical Notes', and how do they assist your interpretation of *The Handmaid's Tale*?

(16) 'Margaret Atwood is preoccupied with the threat and terror of existence in a world apparently lacking in all moral standards and respect for basic human values.' How does *The Handmaid's Tale* work to shock readers into a recognition of the evils of our contemporary world?

(17) 'Writing . . . is an act of faith; I believe it's also an act of hope, the hope that things can be better than they are' (Margaret Atwood). Use this as a starting point to discuss Offred's narrative in *The Handmaid's Tale*.

Specimen answers

(3) Compare and contrast Offred and Moira as feminist heroines in *The Handmaid's Tale*.

The phrase 'feminist heroines' is used here to emphasise women's resistance to male power structures which force women into subordinate positions and deprive them of their rights as human beings. Feminist issues matter in this novel, for it tells the story of an oppressive regime based on Old Testament principles where 'male' is the equivalent of power and sexual potency, and 'female' equals reproduction and submission. It is against this reductive biological view that Offred and Moira raise their voices as hardy survivors of the 1980s. They are the two main examples of feminist positions in the novel (unlike the older women Serena Joy and the Aunts). Yet they are very different from each other, for Offred's resistance always works surreptitiously and through compromise, whereas Moira is a rebel, a dare-devil and a lesbian. Offred represents Atwood's version of a moderate heterosexual feminism in contrast to Moira's separatist feminism.

The careers of the two young women are traced in Offred's narrative. They progress almost in counterpoint, and though we do not know for sure what happens to either of them (both are 'Missing Persons' by the time *The Handmaid's Tale* is made public) it looks as if Offred escaped while Moira did not. It is a bleak ending to stories about feminist heroines' resistance, showing up the limits of possibility but at the same time asserting the necessity to hope against hope: things will be different though not in these two women's lifetimes.

As the main character and narrator here, Offred is trapped in Gilead as a Handmaid, one of the 'two-legged wombs' valued only for her potential as a surrogate mother to help repopulate an environmentally polluted Gilead. Denied all her individual rights, she loses her citizenship and her name and is known only by the patronymic Of-Fred, derived from the name of her current Commander. Most of the time she is isolated and afraid. Virtually imprisoned in the domestic spaces of the home, usually in her own room, she is allowed out only with a shopping partner and for Handmaids' official excursions like Prayvaganzas and Salvagings.

How does Offred survive this treatment? By telling her story Offred presents herself as a subject (a thinking, telling I), which offers a different perspective from Gilead's view of her as object ('sacred vessel', without a voice and without memory). Offred survives by her covert refusals to conform to Gilead's rules: she refuses to forget her past life when she was a daughter, lover, wife and mother; she refuses to give up hope of escape; she refuses to believe that individuals do not matter and she refuses to give up belief in her own individuality; she refuses to give up friendship; she refuses to give up sexual love. Crucially she refuses to be silenced and her narrative recorded on cassette tapes is the witness to the everyday life of Gilead after it has become part of history as a failed sociological experiment.

In bleak circumstances her refusals generate a story which is more than a record of pain and suffering (though it is that too). In her nightly escapes into memory ('Where should I go? Somewhere good' – Chapter 7), she manages to establish a vivid sense of her own individuality as an 80s free woman with economic independence and a domestic life with Luke and their daughter. She is sceptical and ironic about Gilead, and keeps her wits sharp by always looking for 'tiny peepholes' and testing the limits of the system. Unexpectedly, her story is also very lyrical, with her memories of falling in love and of her lost husband, and her rhapsodies in the summer garden ('Goddesses are possible now and their air suffuses with desire' – Chapter 25). Then there is the edgy eroticism of her illicit love affair with Nick, and her odd relationship with the Commander 'after hours' ('The fact is that I'm his mistress. Men at the top have always had mistresses, why should things be any different now?' – Chapter 26).

Offred's attitude challenges the limits of Gilead's power and her story contains some very subversive elements. Undoubtedly, the most subversive story embedded in her narrative is that of her college friend Moira, the one who was never given a Handmaid's name. Moira, the recklessly courageous heroine, forms a contrast to Offred, who admires her very much: 'I want gallantry from her, swashbuckling, heroism, single-handed combat. Something I lack' (Chapter 38). Offred fondly remembers Moira's outrageousness as a student:

> Moira, sitting on the edge of my bed, legs crossed, ankle on knee, in her purple overalls, one dangly earring, the gold fingernail she wore to be eccentric, a cigarette between her stubby yellow-ended fingers. Let's go for a beer. (Chapter 7)

When Moira is brought into the Rachel and Leah Centre she is still wearing jeans and declares that the place is a 'loony bin' (Chapter 13). Moira's rebellious courage and her repeated attempts to escape from the Centre keep up Offred's spirits, and when she finally does manage to escape and becomes 'a loose woman', all the young women see her as a heroine: 'Nevertheless Moira was our fantasy.

We hugged her to us, she was with us in secret, a giggle; she was lava beneath the crust of daily life' (Chapter 22).

Moira continues to surface in Offred's narrative, bobbing up in memory, until her devastating final appearance at Jezebel's, where Offred spots her on her illicit night out with the Commander. Still outrageous, Moira presents a travesty of feminine allure as a Bunny Girl in a black satin outfit, with a bedraggled tail and most comical ears: 'Attached to her head are two ears, of a rabbit or deer, it's not easy to tell; one of the ears has lost its starch or wiring and is flopping halfway down' (Chapter 37). Behind the comedy, however, is the fact that Moira has not managed to escape after all, and as an unregenerate has been consigned to the brothel, where she tells Offred that she has 'three or four good years' ahead of her, drinking and smoking as a Jezebel hostess, before she is sent to the Colonies. Our last view of Moira is on that evening: 'I'd like her to end with something daring and spectacular, some outrage, something that would befit her. But as far as I know that didn't happen' (Chapter 38).

Moira is one of the spirited feminist heroines, like Offred's mother and Offred's predecessor in the Commander's house who left the message in dog Latin scrawled in the cupboard. The sad fact is that these women do get sent off to the Colonies or commit suicide, which Offred herself refuses to do.

Offred and Moira are both feminist heroines, showing women's energetic resistance to the Gilead system, but there are no winners. Neither compromise nor rebellion wins freedom, though it is likely that Offred is rescued by Nick. However, their value lies in their speaking out against the imposition of silence, challenging tyranny and oppression. Their stories highlight the actions of two individual women whose very different private assertions become exemplary or symbolic. Their voices survive as images of hope and defiance to be vindicated by history.

---

(10) Offred describes her narrative as 'this limping and mutilated story'. How does this image relate to *either* the content *or* the structure of *The Handmaid's Tale?*

This metaphor of a wounded human body painfully dragging itself along is used by Offred to describe both her narrative and the social conditions of Gilead in which it takes place. While the painful events within her first-person account of life in a police state could be discussed, with its hanged bodies on the Wall, its attacks by the secret police in the clear light of day, or the fearful event of the Salvaging when even the Handmaids are implicated in murder, attention will be focused here on the fragmented narrative structure, with its isolated scenic units, its gaps and blanks, its narrator's hesitations and doubts, and its dislocations in time sequence.

Offred's comment underlines her own self-consciousness as a story-teller who is aware of the possible responses of her readers. She addresses us directly as in a personal letter: '*Dear You*, I'll say. Just *you*, without a name' (Chapter 7). Telling the story from her own perspective and from her limited knowledge, Offred's emphasis throughout is on process and reconstruction. Of her meetings with the Commander, she says, 'Maybe I should have thought about that at the time, but I didn't. As I said, this is a reconstruction' (Chapter 23). Of her first love-making with Nick she says, 'It didn't happen that way either. I'm not sure how it happened; not exactly. All I can hope for is a reconstruction' (Chapter 40). She has already warned us at the beginning of Chapter 23, 'All of it is a reconstruction. It's a reconstruction now, in my head, as I lie flat on my single bed'.

Telling her story from memory, Offred continually shifts the time sequence as she moves from the present time back into the past by means of flashbacks. She operates by a process of association of ideas, so that her flashes of memory relate (usually by contrast) to her lived experience. They occur as scenic units, sometimes incomplete as they interrupt her daily routines, and sometimes very sustained when she takes her 'time out' in the evenings to remember her mother and Moira and her husband Luke and her daughter, all of whom have now vanished. The novel is an elegy to these missing persons as well as a personal record.

As readers we are plunged into an unfamiliar world at the Rachel and Leah Centre, and only gradually does Offred build up a picture of her daily life in Gilead. Written about the present moment and without awareness of what will happen, Offred's narrative does not have a strong forward-moving plot. It exists instead as an accumulation of crises, and any suspense that might be generated is dispelled by the inconclusive ending. From her own story we do not know if Offred escaped or whether she was taken to prison in the black van, though the 'Historical Notes' give us reason to hope that she was rescued by Nick.

Strong features of Offred's 'limping' narrative are her own doubts and revisions, as she learns more about the Commander and his Wife, for example, so that she never presents a definitive and complete picture of either of them. Similarly, the narrative 'limps' when she reaches limits of knowledge about what happens to Moira, or the details of Ofglen's and her own predecessor's suicides by hanging. However, by embedding in her narrative the stories of all these others, Offred constructs a mosaic of different women's lives under Gilead and their complex responses to their predicament, which range from acquiescence (for example, Serena Joy, Janine) to active collaboration (the Aunts) to outright defiance (for example, her mother and Moira). Not only is Offred's story a chronicle of a Handmaid's life but it is also a witness to the multiplicity that is masked by Gilead's master version of women's submissiveness.

The story may be told in a discontinuous manner but in one respect it has a strong continuity, and that is Offred's voice. This is characterised by her tone of witty scepticism and by her language, with its particular range of organic imagery. The 'body' of the quotation in the title of this essay belongs to one of these image clusters which direct attention to the humanness of the inhabitants of any police state. Offred never forgets that both oppressors and victims have physical bodies and feelings, and through her dislocated narrative she insists on drawing readers' attention to the very qualities of being human that the system excludes, but which offer the only possible means of survival.

Perhaps the crucial point is that despite all her breaks and hesitations, Offred insists on telling her story to her unknown listeners ('I keep on going with this sad and hungry and sordid, this limping and mutilated story, because after all I want you to hear it, as I will hear yours too if I ever get the chance' – Chapter 41). She tells it in secret and in defiance of the regime which demands total silence and submission. It is her story which survives the demise of Gilead and which finally exceeds the limits that Gilead tried to impose.

**(15) What is the function of the 'Historical Notes', and how do they assist your interpretation of *The Handmaid's Tale?*

The 'Historical Notes' are not part of Offred's narrative, but they are part of the novel and they function as a necessary supplement to her story, helping us to put one woman's autobiographical record into historical perspective.

Told by a male narrator, Professor Pieixoto from the University of Cambridge, at an academic conference two hundred years after Offred tells her story, the 'Historical Notes' introduce another futuristic scenario which is different from the story of Gilead. At the University of Denay, Nunavit, up in Arctic Canada, women and Native peoples obviously have some status, for the Chair is a woman professor, Maryann Crescent Moon, and the conference participants go on nature walks and eat fish from the sea (Arctic Char), which suggests a very different social and ecological environment from Gilead.

However, Professor Pieixoto's jokes and his evident interest in the political power structures of Gilead suggest that the old sexist attitudes have not changed very much in two hundred years. His masculinist view leads him to reconstruct the social theory of Gilead and to compare its system with many other examples of tyranny: 'As I have said elsewhere, there was little that was truly original with or indigenous to Gilead: its genius was synthesis.' He establishes a historical context for Offred's narrative, just as he gives a detailed account of how her story was recovered from old cassette tapes made between the 1960s and the 1980s: 'In general, each tape begins with two or three songs, as camouflage, no doubt: then the music is broken off and the speaking voice takes over.'

For all his mass of social data, it is arguable that the professor neglects the most crucial element in this story: Offred herself. Accepting that her name is probably a pseudonym, he does not seem to be as interested in finding out her identity as he is in establishing the identity of her Commander. He offers two possible identifications: Waterford, who 'possessed a background in market research', or the more sinister figure of Judd, who was involved with the CIA. Offred has already told us that her Commander was in 'market research' (Chapter 29), but Professor Pieixoto does not seem to regard her testimony as reliable. In his effort to authenticate Offred's account he is determined to seek external confirmation. Frustrated by the gaps in her narrative, he keeps drawing attention to the things she has not told us:

> She could have told us much about the workings of the Gileadean empire, had she had the instincts of a reporter or a spy. What would we not give, now, for even twenty pages or so of printout from Waterford's private computer!

He does not take notice of what she has chosen to tell, a tale of the suffering and oppression of all women and most men in Gilead. (This might indeed be construed by us as 'the workings of the Gileadean empire'!) The result is that when he says, 'we must be cautious about passing moral judgement upon the Gileadeans. Surely we have learned by now that such judgements are of necessity culture-specific . . . Our job is not to censure but to understand', we as readers may well react against his opinion. Understanding what life in Gilead was like is precisely what he fails to do. And for all his research, he never finds out what happened to Offred, which is what we most want to know. We suspect that for him she was not important enough.

The change in voice from Offred's personal, subjective account to Professor Pieixoto's generalised academic discourse forces us to take up a moral position on what we have just read, to become engaged readers, participants in the action. The novel ends on a question which invites us to enter the debate, having heard two opposite perspectives on the story. This is the point at which Atwood's novel assumes the didactic tone which is a distinctive mark of anti-utopian (dystopian) fiction, as it moves beyond the confines of an imagined world to become a warning to us of a future to be avoided in real life.

Part 5

Suggestions for further reading

The text

ATWOOD, MARGARET: *The Handmaid's Tale*, Virago, London, 1987.

Background reading

ATWOOD, MARGARET: *Poems, 1976–1986*, Virago, London, 1992.

ATWOOD, MARGARET: *Second Words: Selected Critical Prose*, Anansi, Toronto, 1982.

THE BIBLE, especially The Book of Genesis (see also Alexander Cruden, *A Concordance to the Old and New Testaments*, ed. C. S. Carey, Routledge, London, 1925, and Robert Young, *Analytical Concordance to the Holy Bible* 7th edn, Religious Tract Society, London, 1916).

HUMM, MAGGIE (Ed.): *Feminisms: A Reader*, Harvester-Wheatsheaf, Hemel Hempstead, 1992.

INGERSOLL, EARL G. (Ed.): *Margaret Atwood: Conversations*, Virago, London, 1992.

KUMAR, KRISHAN: *Utopianism*, Open University Press, Milton Keynes, 1991.

ORWELL, GEORGE: *Nineteen Eighty-Four*, Penguin, Harmondsworth, 1954.

Critical studies

FULLBROOK, KATE: *Free Women: Ethics and Aesthetics in Twentieth-Century Women's Fiction*, Harvester-Wheatsheaf, Hemel Hempstead, 1990. See Chapter 7 which discusses Atwood's concern with violence and the political dimensions of her fiction.

HOWELLS, CORAL ANN: *Private and Fictional Words: Canadian Women Novelists of the 1970s and 1980s*, Methuen, London and New York, 1987. See Chapter 3 for a fairly straightforward discussion of Atwood's Canadianness and of continuities of theme in *The Handmaid's Tale* and her previous novel *Bodily Harm*.

HUTCHEON, LINDA: *The Canadian Postmodern: A Study of Contemporary English-Canadian Fiction*, Oxford University Press,

Oxford, 1988. See Chapter 7 which discusses Atwood's fiction as Canadian, feminist and postmodernist.

RIGNEY, BARBARA HILL: *Margaret Atwood*, Macmillan Women Writers, London, 1987. A good full-length study of Atwood's work up to and including *The Handmaid's Tale*.

ROOKE, CONSTANCE: *Fear of the Open Heart: Essays on Contemporary Canadian Writing*, Coach House Press, Toronto, 1989. This contains two excellent essays – one on Atwood's imagery and one on ways of interpreting *The Handmaid's Tale*.

When you have read the novel (*and not before*) it may be a good idea to watch the film version of *The Handmaid's Tale*, now available on video. Compare and contrast the novel and the film, highlighting their differences.

The author of these notes

CORAL ANN HOWELLS is a Reader in Canadian Literature at the University of Reading and President of the British Association for Canadian Studies. Educated in Australia, she obtained her Ph D from the University of London. She was Visiting Professor at the University of Guelph, Ontario, Canada, 1981–2. Her main interests are in women's writing from the eighteenth-century Gothic novel to new literatures in English, especially contemporary Canadian fiction. She has lectured in Britain, Europe, Canada, the United States, India and Australia. Her books include *Love, Mystery and Misery; Feeling in Gothic Fiction* (1978), *Private and Fictional Words: Canadian Women Novelists of the 1970s and 1980s* (1987) and *Jean Rhys* (1991), and she is co-editor of *Narrative Strategies in Recent Canadian Literature* (1991). She is currently writing a critical study of Margaret Atwood's fiction.